# Redemption Through Forgiveness

### How God Used My Mental Illness to Save Me

## LISA SLATON

TouchPoint Faith
an imprint of TouchPoint Press

REDEMPTION THROUGH FORGIVENESS: How God Used My Mental Illness to Save Me
By Lisa Slaton
Published by TouchPoint Faith, a TouchPoint Press imprint
Brookland, AR 72417
www.touchpointpress.com

ISBN 13: 978-1-946920-73-7
ISBN 10: 1-946920-73-8

TouchPoint Press books may be purchased in bulk or at special discounts for sales promotions, gifts, fund-raising, or educational purposes. For details, contact the Sales and Distribution Staff: info@touchpointpress.com or via fax: 870-200-6702.

All scripture taken from the New King James version unless otherwise noted.

Editor: Ashley Carlson
Cover Design: Andria Villanueva
Cover image: Kevin Carden, Adobe Stock

Visit the author at LisaSlaton.com

First Edition

Printed in the United States of America.

Disclaimer: This book contains mention of suicide, sexual abuse, and other aspects of mental illness.

# One

The second time I tried to commit suicide I was determined to get the job done.

I opened my bottle of medication and looked inside to see how many pills were in it. It was not a full prescription, but enough pills remained to achieve my desired result. I dumped the pills into my hand and reached for a glass of water. Before I could get the pills into my mouth, my hand opened and tipped the pills onto the floor in front of me.

*I am tired of this. One of you can save Lisa this time.*

I heard the voice, but there was nobody else in the room with me. I dropped to my knees and scrambled to pick up the pills. I felt resistance, but I was not going to let that resistance stop me this time. I was going to silence the voices in my head forever.

*It is no use. We are not strong enough to save Lisa this time. She does not have one ounce of will left to live. We are all going to die.*

I crammed the pills into my mouth and began to swallow them. I nearly choked on them, but I knew that if I did not consume them quickly, there was a good chance I would lose consciousness before I could get them down my throat. I had far more fear of living than I had of dying.

*Now she has done it!*

I tried to ignore the voices as I laid down in bed and waited to die. My eyes fell upon a battered looking doll laying on the pillow beside me. It did not belong to me, and I had no clue how it had gotten there. I pushed it off the bed and closed my eyes. It would all be over soon. I had enough of the voices, the toys, and the accusations of odd behaviors that I could not remember.

I had never given much thought to death. I assumed that it was nothing more than a permanent state of sleep. I would cease to exist. I would finally have the peace that I could never find in life. Only death could eradicate the constant noise in my head.

Fifteen minutes later, I was still waiting to die. Why was I still alive? Why was death taking so long? Maybe I needed more pills. I remembered that my mother kept her pain pills and various other prescription pills in the bathroom cabinet. With a heavy sigh, I got out of my bed and headed towards the bathroom. I would take every pill that I could find no matter what it was. Surely, that would do me in.

I was a few feet from the bathroom door when I felt my body begin to lock up. My arms shot out in front of me, and I could not put them down. My fingers curled up as though I was holding a tennis ball and I could not let go. My head snapped backward, and I could not move it forward. My mouth opened. My jaw opened so wide that pain stabbed my face. I tried to close my mouth, but I could not do it. My leg stiffened up, and my toes curled up like my fingers. Every muscle in my body was stiffening and painfully contracting by themselves. I had no control over any of the movements. A feeling of helpless terror washed over me. This was not the peaceful descent into death that I had anticipated. My body was going haywire, and it was painful and frightening. I could feel my heart banging against my chest. Breathing became a struggle. I heard my body hit the floor with a loud thud.

"What was that?" From somewhere far away I could hear my mother's voice, and I knew she was near me. I tried to tell her what I had done to myself, but my jaw was still wide open and locked in place. Pain shot through my jaw, and I could feel saliva dripping from the side of my mouth. "I think she needs to go to the hospital," was the last thing I heard my mother say.

~

I winced away from the bright light shining on my face. I could see a nurse standing over me shining a flashlight into my eyes. From somewhere behind me I could hear beeping noises. "What are you doing?" I asked, but I could hardly speak due to the soreness in my jaw and face muscles.

"Checking your pupils," the nurse said curtly. She shoved the small flashlight into her uniform pocket and gave me a stern look. "You're a lucky girl," she said.

"I don't feel lucky," I moaned. "My muscles are so sore that I can't move. Why am I so sore?"

"Those were muscle contractions you had," the nurse said. "Contractions and convulsions. Bad." She clicked her tongue.

"What is that beeping noise?" I asked.

"You're hooked up to a heart monitor. All of your muscles were contracting. Your heart is a muscle, too." The nurse began to fuss with the blanket on my bed.

I licked my dry lips. "Can I have some water?" I asked.

The nurse shook her head. "The doctor says nothing by mouth right now," she said. "You will go home today."

"How can I go home?" I wailed. "My muscles are so stiff that I can't even move my legs, much less walk."

"We will put you in a wheelchair and wheel you to the front door. Then you will have to figure it out," the nurse said. "You have been here in the intensive care unit for two days, and you are not in danger anymore."

"I cannot walk!" I retorted. Even though I was frightened about what had happened to me, I was disappointed that I was still alive. I did not want to go back to my life. I would have to try to end my life a third time, and next time, I would find a gun. I was not going to mess it up ever again.

The nurse wrapped a blood pressure cuff on my arm. "You've been here for two days, and you have no insurance," she said. "You already have

a big bill to pay. The powers that be are not going to keep you any longer when you are not in danger if you don't have insurance."

I was incredulous. "Is that the most important thing right now?" I cried out. "Doesn't anybody care what just happened to me?"

"That you tried to knock yourself off?" The nurse pulled the cuff off my arm. "Why did you do it anyway?"

"I hate my life. I don't want to live anymore." I turned my head away from her.

"Many people hate their lives," the nurse said. "They don't run around trying to end it. Only people who feel sorry for themselves do that."

Now I was angry. How dare the nurse say that to me?

Finished with our conversation, the nurse headed towards the door. At the doorway, she paused and then turned to look at me one last time. "Don't you think suicide is a sin?" she asked.

I was not sure what she meant, so I made no response.

"Do you believe in God?" she said with a slight tone of impatience.

"God?" I repeated dumbly. "I don't know."

The nurse shook her head again and sighed. It made me feel like a lost cause. After she had gone, I laid there listening to the beeping of the heart machine and wondered what she meant. I did not know anything about God other than the concept of Him being some mythical presence that lives somewhere in the sky. Nobody in my family was religious. At age 19, I had never been to a church, never even heard a children's Bible story. The only time I had heard the word God while growing up was when my parents used it as a swear word. I knew that God had something to do with Christmas and Easter, but holidays did not mean much to my family. God had never been any part of my life. I wondered why this nurse had brought Him up to me. What did she mean by saying suicide was a sin? I was not even sure what sin was. I knew it meant to do something that was wrong, but by whose standards? Who was it that decides what makes something wrong?

Up until that point, I had never thought of killing myself as wrong. It was my life, and I was the author of my own life. It was nobody else's business what I chose to do with my life. Nobody had the right to tell me it was wrong to remove myself from such a wretched and miserable existence. I was 19 years old, and that made me an adult, even though I did not feel like one. I did not have to answer to anybody but myself.

My thoughts about God were quickly forgotten when the doctor on duty came into the room. He picked up my chart and quickly glanced through it before beginning to unhook me from the heart monitor. "You are stable enough to go home," he told me.

I struggled to sit up in the bed. "I don't think I can walk," I said.

The doctor reached out his hand and grasped mine to help pull me up. "It will take several days for your muscles to heal," he said. He stepped back from the bed and frowned at me. "Your chart indicates that this is your second suicide attempt in less than a year," he said. "Since you keep ending up in the hospital it appears as though you really do not want to die and instead you are seeking some attention."

A chorus of jumbled angry voices rose in my head. "That's not true," I said. "I do want to die, but somebody keeps stopping me."

"The only one stopping you is yourself," the doctor said.

I curled up my fists and struck the bed rails. "No!" I cried out. "It's not me. Somebody else is stopping me from dying!"

The doctor shook his head. "Who do you think is stopping you?" he asked.

"I don't know." I covered my eyes with my hand and began to weep. "I can hear the voices, but I can never see the faces."

"If you hear voices you may need different medication," the doctor said.

I wiped my eyes and looked away from him. "The medication does not stop the voices," I said. "Nothing will stop the voices except death."

"Schizophrenia is a treatable condition," the doctor said. "You just need to find the medication that will work best for you. If your psychiatrist does not agree to change your medication, then I suggest you find another doctor. You are too young to die."

"It's not my age that matters. It is my quality of life," I said.

"At nineteen years old, you should not feel that the quality of your life is bad enough to want to die," the doctor said. "I will fill out your discharge papers. The nurse will call your parents and let them know that you will be discharged."

I felt my heart begin to beat frantically in my chest. "Please don't call my parents," I begged. "I can't go back with my mother."

The doctor looked annoyed. "Where else can you go?" he asked.

"Anywhere except with them," I pleaded.

"There is nowhere else for you to go. The nurse will call them," the doctor said. Before I could protest further, he turned on his heel and quickly left the room.

*Thanks for nothing! That is quackery at its finest.*

I covered my ears, but I knew it would not silence the voices.

*We could run away and live in the woods.*

The voice sounded like that of a child, and I suddenly had a strong urge to put my thumb into my mouth. I put my hands underneath the blanket. Too many people had already caught me with my thumb in my mouth. With a heavy sigh, I leaned back against the pillow and began to consider my next suicide attempt. It was inevitable that I would try again.

*What did that nurse mean when she asked if Lisa believes in God? Who is God?* The child's voice was soft and whispery.

*I do not know much about God, honey. I think He created the world. I think He lives in a church.*

*God does not live in a church, silly. He lives way up in the sky, higher than the clouds. His home is in heaven.*

I did my best to ignore the conversation that was occurring in my head as I tried to decide what to do with my life. Diagnosed with schizophrenia the year before, I had given up on ever being able to live a normal life. Even if I were able to escape my dysfunctional family, I would not be able to survive on my own while struggling with so many psychiatric symptoms. The medication that I was taking to combat the voices and hallucinations had not decreased them in any way. I wondered about the doctor's suggestion that I needed to try a different medication. I doubted I had the effort to give different medication a chance.

*Do we have to go back to that house? I do not want to go back there. I hate Lisa's mother.*

*We must go back there for a while, but we will have to figure something else out soon if there is any chance of saving Lisa.*

"Why do you keep saving me?" I lashed out. "I don't want to be saved. Leave me alone!"

A nursing assistant stuck her head in the door. "Do you need anything?" she asked.

I felt my face burn with embarrassment. "No," I said.

"You can get up and get dressed," she said. "You are being discharged."

I tried to move my legs and hesitated. "Could you help me?" I asked. "My muscles hurt so much that I don't think I can manage to do it on my own."

A look of annoyance crossed the nursing assistant's face. "I'm busy right now," she said.

I tried to move my legs again and winced from the pain. "I don't think I can do it," I said.

With a heavy sigh, the nursing assistant came into the room. She grabbed both of my legs and roughly pulled them off the bed.

"Ow!" I cried out.

"I do not have sympathy for people who try to commit suicide," the nursing assistant snapped. "You kind of people are selfish. My sister tried that and nearly destroyed my family."

I swallowed hard and lowered my eyes to the floor. "I'm sorry," I said. I did not know if I was apologizing for her sister or myself.

The assistant yanked open the closet door and pulled out a bag containing my clothes. I reached out and took the bag from her. "I think I can get myself dressed," I told her.

The assistant put her hands on her hips and glared at me. "What were you going to tell God when you met Him?" she demanded. "Were you going to tell Him that you did not appreciate the life that He gave you?"

I clutched the bag to my chest and stared at her. Here was another person bringing up the subject of God to me. Thinking about God twice in one day was probably more than I had ever thought about Him in my entire life. "If God gave me my life then yes, I would tell Him that I don't appreciate it," I replied. "But I was not thinking about God at all. I was only thinking about escaping my life."

"What is so bad about your life that you would be bold enough to drop in on the Lord God Almighty without an invitation?" the assistant asked.

Startled by this second conversation about God, I was unable to become angry with the assistant for prying into my personal life. I thought I was going to die and have an eternal peaceful sleep. I had not thought about dealing with God or anything else. I was not sure that I believed in God. I did not know enough about Him to have formed an opinion either way. God was not an important issue in my life at that point.

The nursing assistant's eyes searched mine as she waited for an answer. "I have schizophrenia," I told her, even though I did not think it was any of her business. "I have a bad home life. I have been abused in many ways and— "

The assistant raised her hand to stop me. "Nothing is too bad to hand over to God," she said.

I began to feel frustrated. "I do not have a clue what you are talking about," I said.

At that moment, a nurse passed by and called into the room, "Maria, we need you in room four stat."

"I have to go," the nursing assistant said. "I will be back shortly with a wheelchair to bring you downstairs to the front door."

I lifted my right leg and shook my foot. "I think I can walk now," I said.

"It's hospital policy that we roll you to the door. Wait for me here," the assistant said as she hurried out of the door.

I sank into the chair next to the bed and slowly began the painful process of getting dressed. In my head, I could hear the distant sound of jumbled voices, but this time I could not make out what they were saying. My mind flittered from thoughts of God to my mother. I did not want to see her. I did not want to go back home, but my only alternative would be to become homeless. My mother was not going to appreciate that I tried to commit suicide again. The last time I had tried it, she screamed at me for making her look bad, and then she yelled at me for failing. I was a failure in every way imaginable in her eyes.

The nursing assistant returned to my room twenty minutes later with a wheelchair in tow. She spoke not a word to me as she rolled me into the elevator and downstairs to the front door. As I was walking out of the front door, she called to me, "May God forgive you!"

I turned my head to face her. "Forgive me for what?" I called back to her.

"For your sins," she said, as the automatic door closed to separate us.

I shook my head and turned away. For what sins did I need forgiveness? Life had been cruel to me so far. I should be the one doing the forgiving, not the other way around. I took a deep breath and filled my lungs with fresh air. The sky above me was a brilliant blue. I began to wonder about the meaning of life. Was there any meaning to it? Were some people like myself born to know only misery, and then to die at a young age?

In my peripheral vision, I caught a glimpse of a child standing beside me staring at me. I began to feel enveloped in a dark feeling of sadness and emptiness. The child had long black hair and a pale complexion. I turned my head to look at her, to share in her despair, but she was gone as quickly as she had appeared. 'It's just another one of my hallucinations,' I thought sourly.

I saw my father's old car pull into the parking lot, and I breathed a sigh of relief to find that my mother was not with him. I would face her wrath when I arrived home, but at least the ride there would be peaceful. I had an awkward and distant relationship with my father, so I knew that he would feel too uncomfortable to speak with me about what had happened.

I climbed into the car and placed my head against the headrest. I was contemplating my next suicide attempt, but now something was nagging

me that I could not quite figure out. The hospital staff had put concerns in my head about death and God.

I was not sure how to find further information about God, and I was not sure that I was interested in finding out more anyway. I had a more pressing matter to deal with at that moment. I needed to figure out how I was going to protect myself from my mother's wrath once I got home.

# Two

*Though I walk in the midst of trouble, You will
revive me; You will stretch out your hand against
the wrath of my enemies, and Your right hand will
save me. (Psalm 138:7)*

Two weeks after I left the hospital, I sat in my bedroom feeling depressed and engaging in self-mutilation. I found that cutting my arms and legs with broken glass or making circular burns on my skin with a car cigarette lighter was an adequate way to release my pent-up anger. Around my house, children were to be seen and not heard, and I had learned to bury my emotions. Self-mutilation was not an act of attention for me. Even though it was the middle of summer, I wore long sleeves and long pants to hide my handiwork. Nobody bothered to question why I dressed in such a way in the sweltering weather.

I was poised to drag a piece of glass along my arm when something caught my eye. Taped to the wall above my bed were two pictures that were not there that morning. One of the pictures, eloquently done in brilliant bright colors, was a picturesque scene of flowers, trees, and birds under a bright smiling sun. The word "Mouse" in childish scrawl was in the bottom left-hand corner.

The second picture was in stark contrast to the happy one. Colored with only black and gray crayons, it looked to be a long-toothed monster chasing a group of stick-figure children. The background contained only barren, black trees. The word "Bug" adorned the black sky.

Beads of sweat began to form on my forehead as I looked at those pictures. I did not know who drew them or when they had ended up on my wall. If my mother saw the pictures, they would undoubtedly lead to questions that I would not be able to answer. I wanted to tear down the pictures and stuff them into the garbage, but I felt a measure of respect for them that I did not understand. Carefully I pulled them from the wall and placed them into the bottom drawer of my dresser, where I had hidden other childish items that I had found at random times in my bedroom. I did not know to whom any of it belonged, but I thought I might find the owner of all of it one day.

With the pictures hidden from view, my bedroom felt safe again. I sat down on my bed and tried to figure out when the drawings had ended up on the wall. I found that chunks of time were often missing from my memory. I could go for hours or days without being able to remember where I was or what I was doing. The lapses in time and memory were frightening, but I had become an expert in hiding my confusion about them around other people. I assumed all of it was just the usual symptoms of schizophrenia.

The sound of footsteps approaching interrupted my thoughts, and I felt my body tense with anxiety. Relief washed over me when I heard a knock on the door. My mother would never knock. She would barge right in.

"Phone call for you," my brother hollered from the other side of the door. "Some girl named Tina."

I was stunned. I never got phone calls because I had no friends. In grade school, I was bullied by most of the other children. In high school, I tried to stay to myself, but there was a girl named Tina that I would sometimes talk to. She would sit with me for lunch, and we would be outcasts together. I never thought that I would hear from Tina after we graduated. I did not want to hear from her. I felt bothered. I wondered how she had gotten my phone number. "Hello?"

"Lisa, how are you doing?" Tina's voice was cheerful.

I felt annoyed by the unwanted intrusion of the phone call. I had a low tolerance for engaging with people. Being around people for as much as ten minutes left me feeling mentally exhausted. "How did you get my phone number?" I demanded.

"Phonebook," Tina said. "Is it a secret?"

"No," I sighed. "I'm sorry. Why are you calling me?"

"I thought we were friends," Tina said.

"We've been out of school for over a month," I said." I have not spoken to you since then."

Tina ignored my implication. "I have a proposal for you," she said. "How would you like a job?"

I struggled to make sense of that. "What do you mean?" I asked.

"Do you want a job?" Tina repeated. "Everybody gets a job when they finish school. I have been working at that nursing home over in Alton. My mother is the Director of Nursing there, and she is in desperate need of some nursing assistants to help take care of the elderly residents. That is what I am doing there. They do not pay much more than minimum wage, but it is not bad for a first job. They do have some benefits, like health insurance. I thought of you right away. I already spoke to my mother about you. She says if you're interested you can stop by the nursing home on Monday and talk to her about it."

It took me a minute to find my voice. "Thank you for the offer," I said. My voice trembled with fear. "I will think about it."

What was there to think about? It was absurd to think I could work. I had never thought about working. I was so depressed most of the time that I rarely thought about my future. Besides that, I did not like being around people. My self-esteem was so far in the garbage that I had trouble even looking people in the eye. My mother always called me ugly and worthless, and I more than believed her. It was my habit to look down to avoid people seeing how ugly I was. How could I even entertain the idea of working in my current state? I would inevitably fail on day one and make a laughingstock of myself. The mere thought of trying to talk to Tina's mother about anything made me feel sick with fear. There was no way. I could not do it.

I hung up the phone and returned to my bedroom. It took every bit of my effort to lift my eyes and look at myself in the mirror that was hanging on my wall. Due to my depression, I had not bathed or washed my hair in over a week. My hair was greasy and hung limply around my face. I looked old. I felt old. *I am ugly*, I thought. *Ugly and worthless, just like my mother says. I'm so tired. Everything is such an effort.*

From somewhere outside of my bedroom I could hear the house becoming trashed as my parents fought with each other. I wondered how would be to have just one day of peace. I sat down on my bed and dared to allow myself to wonder. What would it be like to have a job and make money like a normal person? Could people with schizophrenia hold down a job? Could I possibly be brave enough to try to talk to Tina's mother about it? From somewhere deep inside of me, I felt pushed to try it, even though I felt terrified by the thought of it. It felt like the choice was taken out of my hands. I had no idea why or what would happen, but I knew I had to force myself to talk to Tina's mother on Monday. Despite myself, I was going to make myself do it. With a heavy sigh, I summoned up every small bit of effort I could find and gathered some clean clothes to take a bath. I did not know it at the time, but that phone call from Tina was going to bring some significant changes into my life.

~

I did not have to go through an official job interview. Even though I had zero work experience, Tina's mother was so desperate for nursing assistants that she hired me on the spot. Less than ten minutes after arriving I found myself with a job. Tina's mother showed me the floor that I would be working on and talked to me about what would be expected of me.

The sights and the sounds in the nursing home were overwhelming to me. There were beeping noises and the sounds of the staff chattering.

Some of the elderly residents sitting in wheelchairs along the walls were moaning and calling out "Nurse! Please help me!"

I reached out to touch one of the people who was crying out for help, but my compassion gave way to fear and curiosity. I recoiled my hand and shoved it into my pocket. The voices rose up in my head.

*Do not be afraid, honey. These people need help. Maybe Lisa can help them.*

At the end of the hallway, I could see the familiar sight of the long-haired solemn-faced little girl. Her body was trembling, and her pale hands covered her face. It was the first time that I had seen her when other people were around me. Usually, I only saw the children whenever I was alone.

I forced myself to look away from the child and tried to focus on what Tina's mother was saying to me. The jumble of voices in my head made it difficult to concentrate on what was going on around me. I heard the excitement, giggling, and crying all rolled into one sound.

"You'll help them with their daily activities such as bathing, toileting, and eating," Tina's mother said. "You will work with another nursing assistant because you are not legally certified. If you decide that you would like to continue your employment with us, you will have to take a class to become certified. We will pay for that class, provided you sign an agreement to remain employed here for six months upon completion of your certification."

It was at that moment when I became completely overwhelmed with the situation. Although I wanted that job more than anything else in the world, my confidence bottomed out. There was no way that I could hold a job when I was fraught with hallucinations and so many other bizarre behaviors. What was I thinking? I was likely to lose the job within the first hour. I could not take care of other people when I could barely take care of myself. Considering the volume of psychotic symptoms that I constantly struggled with, it was unlikely that my psychiatrist would approve of my trying to hold a job. It was beyond ludicrous that I was there talking to Tina's mother about it.

The voices became clear in my head. *Lisa is wimping out. We cannot let her wimp out now. If she has a job, she can make money and get us all out of the hellhole that we are living in.*

*Never mind Lisa. I will take over and do the job myself.*

*You cannot work a job. I do not think any of us can. Lisa is the smartest, and she has the most capability.*

*I beg your pardon. I beg to differ!*

Eclipsed by the voices in my head, all the other sounds around me began to fade in and out. It was too much for me. I felt my world turning to black, and I knew I was going to lose consciousness. It was inevitable. The last words I heard before I went into the darkness were *one of us must help Lisa!*

The next time I opened my eyes, I was standing in my bedroom, and my brother Brian was standing in front of me. "Now that you have a job, I will sell you one of my cars," he was saying to me. "It is too far for you to walk there and back."

I struggled against confusion and tried to regain my composure. I had no recollection of what had happened at the nursing home or how I had gotten myself home. I desperately tried to recall what had transpired, but all that I could see in my mind was a vast black space.

"Do you want the car?" Brian asked. "I will sell it to you for a thousand. You can make payments."

I shook my head to clear it. "I don't need the car," I said. "I do not have a job. I turned it down."

Brian looked as confused as I felt. "What are you talking about?" he said. "You just told me that you start your job on Monday morning!"

I was shocked. That could not be possible. "I told you I have a job?" I said. "What else did I tell you about it?"

Brian gave me an incredulous look. "Have you lost your mind again?" he said.

"Tell me everything that you heard me say," I begged.

Brian shook his head and let out a low whistle. "I wonder what is wrong with you sometimes," he remarked. "It's almost as if you have dementia or some other memory impairment."

"Please!" I exclaimed. "This is very important. I need to know what I said to you."

Brian's forehead wrinkled with concentration as he tried to recall what I had told him. "You came home excited," he said. "You said you have to be at your job at seven o'clock on Monday morning, and that you have to find some white clothing to wear until you get a proper uniform."

I felt the blood drain from my face as I backed away from Brian and sank onto my bed. I was too confused and overwhelmed to feel excited. I had completed my interaction with Tina's mother at the nursing home, but I had zero recollection of what had happened. Somehow, I had managed to secure the job, but how in the world was I going to perform it?

"Are you alright?" Brian asked with a touch of concern in his voice. "You should still be excited about having your first job. Maybe Mom will finally be pleased with you."

"She will never be pleased with me," I said. "She hates me."

"I think Mom hates everybody," Brian said.

"She hates me in particular," I said. "She claims that I ruined her life when I was born."

"I wouldn't pay attention to that," Brian said lightly. "So, do you want to buy my car or not?"

I could not believe that in two weeks' time I had gone from a serious suicide attempt to having my first job and a car. How had that happened? I still was not sure that I was going to remain alive from one day to the next. "I will buy it," I told him.

Later that evening, I received another call from Tina. I hated getting phone calls, but I was glad that she did call because I needed more information about what had transpired between her mother and me. I patiently listened as Tina rattled on details about the job and gossip about the staff. The more that she talked, the more anxiety I felt. I tried to tell her that I changed my mind about working, but the words would not come out of my mouth. Although Tina and I knew each other from high school, she did not know about my struggle with mental illness, and she knew next to nothing about my family life. I was an expert at keeping secrets.

Our conversation about work was winding down when Tina said, "Enjoy your day tomorrow. It is your last day of freedom. I have the day off, but I am going to church with my mother in the morning."

My ears immediately perked up. "You never told me that you go to church," I said.

"My mother insists that I go," Tina laughed. "If I had any say about it, I would sleep late in the morning. Does your family go to church?"

"No," I said, and for some reason, I felt a tinge of embarrassment, as if it were wrong to admit that we did not attend church.

"Would you like to come with us in the morning?" Tina asked. "My mother would be glad to pick you up. She would probably drive a hundred miles if it meant that she could take somebody to church."

I hesitated. A small part of me was tempted to agree to go to see what the God stuff was all about, but I resisted. I was uncomfortable in most social situations. I would not know what to wear or how to act. I feared to make a fool of myself. "I don't think so," I said. "Maybe some other time."

"Okay," Tina said. "Before I let you go, I have a message for you from my mother. She says when you get to work on Monday, go straight to her office. You need to fill out tax forms and other paperwork."

"I don't know how to fill any of that out," I said worriedly.

"It's your first job. My mother will help you with it," Tina assured me. "Good luck."

After I hung up, I thought about Tina inviting me to church. I wondered why I was suddenly running into so many people who were talking about God. He had been an absent topic for the first nineteen years of my life. Why was I suddenly starting to hear so much about Him now?

Brian interrupted my thoughts by handing me the keys to his Oldsmobile. God once again flitted away from my mind as the pressures of my life came back into focus. I had to figure out what I was going to do about the job and about staying alive in general.

# Three

*And we know that all things work together for good to those who love God, to those who are called according to His purpose. (Romans 8:28)*

When I woke up early Monday morning, I could scarcely believe my eyes. The first thing I saw was a huge colorful poster on my wall across from my bed saying, "**Congratulations on your first job!**" A smaller sign was hanging on my door that said, "**You can do it**!" Colorful balloons and streamers adorned my ceiling.

Somebody had been thoughtful enough to decorate my room during the night while I was sleeping. I wondered how they were able to do so much in the room without waking me up. Even though I was a nervous wreck about starting a job, this kindness whichever family member had taken the pains to show me touched my heart. I knew my parents would not have done it, so I assumed that one or both of my brothers had tried to make the morning nice for me.

I sat up in bed and tried to sort out my thoughts. I had less than two hours to decide whether I was going to show up at the job or not. Terrified by the idea of failure and of making a fool out of myself, I was also afraid of the nursing home staff finding out that I had a serious mental illness. I was certain that having a mental illness would immediately disqualify me from having a job where I would be taking care of other people. I did not want to deal with the stigma that I would likely face once my bizarre behaviors and frequent mood swings began to surface in front of the staff as well as the residents.

I decided not to go. I laid back down and pulled the covers over my head.

*Get up! You have to go!*

The voice in my head was urgent, and I felt a force trying to pull my body out of bed. I struggled against the force until my body felt like it was on fire.

*Trust me! You have to go! I think this job will lead to good things for you. Get up and try!*

My legs rose from the bed, and then came crashing back down. I became angry with whatever force was struggling against me, and tears of resentment began flowing down my hot cheeks. "You cannot make me go!" I yelled, not caring who may have heard me. "I am too crazy to hold a job. I will only fail, and everybody in the town will know that I am sick!"

I lost the fight. Whatever was struggling with me soon had my body out of bed and in a standing position. I covered my face with my hands and wept. "Leave me alone," I begged. "I cannot do this. It's too much for me."

I kept pleading, even as I found myself reaching for my white clothes to get dressed. I felt like I was on autopilot. My motions were fluid as I continued to get dressed and comb my hair. I cried and struggled through it all, but the force was stronger than I was.

*Please do not be afraid. I would never do anything that I thought would harm you. I just have a strong feeling that you should go and do this. Don't cry. It hurts us when you cry. It hurts my heart so bad to see your tears.*

I threw my comb onto the floor. "Stop talking to me," I panted. "You are not real. The voices are not real. My doctor told me that the voices are only a symptom of my mental illness. You are not part of reality!"

The force struggling against me ceased, and the voices were temporarily quiet. My shoulders shook from the frustration that I felt. I wiped the tears from my eyes and began moving across my room toward the door. I had only been awake for a short time, and already I felt exhausted. The streamers on my ceiling brushed lightly against my head as I moved forward.

A comforting voice whispered to me, *keep going. Do not give up. There is good there for you. Keep your feet moving one step at a time. You are stronger than you think you are. Just keep moving.*

The tears dried on my face as I kept moving forward. I went downstairs. I was too tired to eat breakfast. My mother was sitting at the kitchen table, already drinking beer at six o'clock in the morning. Perhaps she had never stopped drinking from the night before. She looked at me and said, "You will never make it."

I wondered if my mother could feel the hatred that I had for her. I had no love in my heart for her. I hated her so much that I wished she would die in the most violent way possible. My mother had been cruel and abusive to me my entire life. She blamed me for her own miserable life. She had told me many times that if I had not been born, she would not have been in an unhappy marriage and that she would have possibly made something better out of herself. She put a burden on my shoulders that was almost impossible for me to carry. I spent my childhood feeling guilty for being born. I felt responsible for ruining her life. Her cruelty to me knew no bounds. I hated her guts for it, but I was too frightened to let her know how I felt about her. Showing my hatred would only lead to more cruelty from her. Repressing that amount of hate was eating me up inside and further increased my depression. Trapped by so many negative emotions that I could never express, it left me crippled with headaches and stomach pain.

"You will never make it," my mother repeated as she took a long draw from her cigarette. "You will be as worthless on your job as you were on the day you were born. I don't know why they hired somebody as ugly as you are."

Hearing my mother's words only made me even more reluctant to go. I began to feel so much anxiety that my legs trembled, and my heart raced.

Again, I heard a voice whisper in my head: *never mind what she says. You can do this. All you have to do is keep moving forward. Keep going and see what will happen.*

It was a struggle to get to my car. My feet kept stopping. I wanted to run in the opposite direction. My stomach was in knots.

"I cannot do it," I said aloud to nobody.

*You can do it. Keep moving,* a voice responded.

I made it to my car, only to find that the car would not start. It was a ten-year-old car and not in the best shape. I beat my fists on the steering wheel with frustration. I was right in the center of two forces battling for control of me. Something was trying to prevent me from going to the job while *something else* was trying to get me there. Now I had a real problem. It was too late for me to walk the two miles to work, and I knew I did not have enough energy to walk there.

I lowered my head in defeat. "It's over. I tried. I am going back to bed. I give up," I said.

"What's the matter?" I heard a voice say.

I looked up and found Brian leaning against the car. I was surprised to see him up so early. "You sold me a pile of junk," I told him. "This thing won't start."

My brother laughed at me. "It will start," he said. "I forgot to tell you there is a trick to it. Just jiggle the key upwards a few times. I'll get that ignition switch fixed for you."

I did as he instructed, and the car roared to life. "What are you doing up this early?" I asked him. He was two years younger than I was and had dropped out of high school. "I never see you up this early anymore."

"I don't know why. I opened my eyes, and something told me to get up and come out here. It looks like it's a good thing that I did, or you may have lost your job before you even started it."

"I'm not sure if that's a good thing or a bad thing," I mumbled. I gave Brian a slight smile. "That was nice of you to decorate my room last night," I told him. "How did you manage to do all of that without waking me up? Did you do it in the darkness?"

A look of confusion crossed Brian's face. "I did not decorate your room last night," he said. "I was asleep all night."

"You didn't do all of that decorating in my room last night?" I asked with surprise. "Somebody put streamers and balloons in my room while I was sleeping. Are you certain it was not you?"

"I would know if I did it," Brian said. "It wasn't me."

"Maybe it was Donnie," I said, although I had my doubts. He was only eleven years old, and not very thoughtful. He would not have been able to do all of the decorating without waking me up.

"Nah," Brian said. "Donnie wouldn't do something like that."

"Mom and Dad sure wouldn't do it," I said.

"Nope," Brian agreed. "There you go losing your mind again. You must have done it yourself to make yourself feel good about having a job."

"I didn't do that," I said. "I did not decorate my bedroom."

"A lot of the time when you get stressed you do things, and you do not remember doing them," Brian pointed out. "I thought the medication was supposed to help you with that, but it does not seem to be helping at all." He nodded in the direction of the street. "You better get going, or you will be late on your first day," he said. "Good luck on the first day of your first job. Are you nervous about it?"

The decorations in my bedroom weighed heavily on my mind. "I am not sure what I feel right now," I said. "The way things are already going for me this morning I wonder if I will even make it there without a car accident or something else happening." I put the car into reverse and slowly backed out of the driveway.

~

I began training with another nursing assistant named Tammy. She was five years older than I was and a very bubbly and enthusiastic person. She did not seem to notice how shy and awkward I was with her and the rest of the staff. I found it difficult to look at any of the staff when they were talking to me. As uncomfortable as I was with the staff, however, I was just as comfortable with the residents. I got along well with them, and I relished being able to help them.

I took to becoming a nursing assistant like a fish took to water. It did not bother me to help them with their bathing and toileting unless I had to see one of the men exposed. The years of sexual abuse I had endured from my paternal Grandfather had left me feeling so frightened that I was awkward around them. Despite that, I was able to keep reminding myself that these men were not the ones who had hurt me. Still, the uncomfortable and frightened feelings prevailed, and I avoided seeing the men without clothes on as much as I possibly could. Except for that, I flourished when it came to helping the residents. Somehow, I managed to overcome my depression and lack of energy to care for them. The depression and anxiety were still there, but I was able to distract myself from them temporarily. I was able to put aside the stress of my own life to focus on somebody else's troubles.

A few hours into that first work shift, Tammy told me that she was impressed with me. I was getting along well with the residents, and I was soaking up the knowledge of how to be a nursing assistant like a sponge. In no time flat, I learned how to take vital signs, empty catheter bags, put people on a bedpan, chart in the logbooks, and how to lift and transfer people using the proper techniques. By the fourth hour, I felt ready to work on my own, but because I was not legally certified, I would have to stay paired up with Tammy.

When it came time for my lunch break, I did not want to go. Tammy insisted that I take it. It would be a relief for me to spend a half hour by myself. I went downstairs to the employee break room and was glad to find it unoccupied. I purchased a can of soda and sat at a table in the corner of the room. Now that I was away from the residents, I felt my depression returning, and I wanted to be alone with my thoughts.

A few minutes later I heard the door swing open. A nurse from a different floor entered the room. She was a pretty woman, maybe in her late 50s, wearing a blazing white uniform. She smiled brightly when she saw me. I quickly looked away from her. *Please do not sit with me,* I thought. *Please leave me alone.*

Out of the corner of my eye, I saw her purchase a cup of coffee. Much to my dismay, she approached my table and set directly across from me. I felt annoyed by her intrusion. "Hello," she said, reaching out her hand toward me.

I was startled. I was not about to shake her hand. I did not touch people, nor did I allow people to touch me. The residents were the only exception, and even then, I tried to make the touch dissipate as quickly as possible.

The nurse did not seem slighted by my unwillingness to shake her hand. She withdrew her hand and said, "My name is Gloria. What's yours?"

"Lisa," I scowled.

"Are you new here? I haven't seen you before."

I sighed the biggest sigh that I could muster. My disdain about having Gloria's company was not dissuading her. "Today is my first day," I said.

"Welcome," Gloria said. "I work on the third floor. Where are you?"

"Fourth," I said, staring down at my soda can. Maybe if I did not look at Gloria, she would get the hint that I did not want her there.

"Fourth is a good floor for newcomers," Gloria said cheerfully. "The residents on that floor are easy to deal with. The second floor, that is where most of the skilled care residents are." She paused and took a sip of her coffee. "I have worked here for eight years and have worked on all of the floors," she continued. "You look young. Are you still in school?"

I sighed again. I did not like nosy people. "I'm nineteen," I mumbled.

"I cannot remember what it was like to be that age," Gloria chuckled.

I slowly lifted my head to look at her. My eye caught a shiny gold necklace that she was wearing. The pendant on the chain was a cross with Jesus on it.

When Gloria saw me eyeing her necklace, she reached up and fingered it. "It is a crucifix," she said. "Are you a Christian?"

I quickly averted my eyes and shook my head.

"Are you an atheist then?" she asked.

"I don't know what that is," I said.

"An atheist is a person who doesn't believe God exists," Gloria explained.

"I have never given it much thought one way or the other," I said.

"You haven't?" Gloria sounded surprised. "Maybe it's time that you did."

*Here we go again*, I thought. Gloria was the fourth person to talk about God to me in the past three weeks. "Why?" I asked.

"It's something everybody needs to think about," Gloria replied. "Every person on this earth needs to make a decision where they want to spend eternity after their life here ends."

I thought Gloria might be one of those holy rollers who enjoy pushing religion down other people's throats. I had never met a holy roller, but I had heard it was best to avoid them at all costs. They were fanatics of the worst kind. Still, her words left me curious, and I wanted to know what she was talking about. "I do not believe in life after death," I said. "I believe once you are dead you are gone."

"That is not what it says in the Bible," Gloria said. "The Bible says, not only do you continue to exist after death, but you also go to heaven or hell depending on what choice you made while you were here on this earth."

"I do not know what the Bible says," I admitted. "How do we know it is true? It's just a book."

"You think the Bible is just another book?" Gloria said. She sounded surprised, but there was also an incredible amount of patience in her voice. "The Bible is God's word straight to mankind."

"So, God wrote it?" I asked.

"God did not write it with pen and paper," Gloria replied. "Many different people wrote the Bible at different times in history. Each person who wrote it was inspired by God to write whatever God breathed to them."

"If God exists and the Bible is so important, I would think He would have written it Himself," I said.

Gloria fell silent as she sipped her coffee. I glanced up at her. She was not looking at me, but I could see a troubled look on her face. It occurred to me how outrageous it was that I was debating with a stranger about things I knew next to nothing about. I began to feel awkward about the situation. I was curious about her views on God and death, but I also did not want to hear any more about it. Death had always been a peaceful sense of relief from this life for me. I did not want that ruined with thoughts of an afterlife, and especially not of the thought of going to hell, which I had only seen depicted as a place of fire where the devil resided. I did not believe in the devil any more than I believed in God. As far as I was concerned, both God and the devil were no more than fables handed down for generations by creative-minded people. I did not have the time nor the effort to think about such nonsense. My life was difficult, and I had trouble enough trying to think about how to survive each day. I began to feel angry that I was becoming drawn into this type of conversation. Abruptly, I pushed back my chair and stood up. "I think my break is over," I said. "It's time that I get back to the floor."

"It was very nice meeting you," Gloria said. "I am sure we will run into each other again, and I hope that we can talk more about this. I love it whenever I have the opportunity to talk about God."

*I doubt it,* I thought as I headed for the door.

Gloria stood up and followed me. "Wait a minute," she said. "I want to give you something." She reached into her uniform pocket and then pressed something into my hand. I looked down at it. It was a tiny book with a worn cover that said *Holy Bible* on it. "It's my copy," Gloria said. "I like to read it when I am on my breaks. I want you to have it. I've got more of them at home."

I felt something stir within me. I ran my finger over the cover gingerly. I had never held a Bible before. I had never opened one, much less owned one. Something about it made me feel awe and curiosity. I knew it must be an important book. Suddenly feeling embarrassed, I shoved it into my pocket and headed back up the stairs to my new job.

# Four

*For God so loved the world that He gave His only begotten Son, that whoever believes in Him should not perish but have everlasting life. (John 3:16)*

When I arrived home after my first work shift, I found my father sleeping on the front porch. I knew he was drunk. I stepped over him and tried to get into the door, but it was locked. I reached down and shook my father's shoulder. "Dad!" I shouted. "Wake up."

My dad opened his eyes and looked up at me.

"What happened this time?" I asked.

My father let out a long stream of obscenities. "Your mother locked me out of the house again," he slurred.

My stomach sank. "Again?" I asked. My mother had a fondness for locking my father and me out of the house whenever she was angry, which was most of the time. She would kick us out at any time of the day or night no matter the weather. I spent many nights sleeping curled up against the woodpile in the corner of the yard or wandering around the neighborhood seeking shelter against the brutal winter winds. "Did you hurt her?" I asked.

My father closed his eyes and did not answer. I went to the living room window and peered inside. The house looked trashed, but I could see my mother sitting unharmed in a chair. Knowing that she would not unlock the door and allow us in until she was ready, the only thing I could do was wait it out. I went over to my father's car and climbed into the front seat to wait there.

I forgot about my first day of work as I sat in the car and wrestled with anxiety. I was worried sick that the frequent violence between my parents would wind up leaving somebody in the house dead. Slapping and punching had long ago graduated into stabbing each other with knives and breaking each other's bones. Whenever one of them landed in the hospital, they would lie about what had happened. They never pressed charges against each other.

I was not so much worried about my parents killing each other as I was about something happening to one of my brothers or me. My mother frequently threatened to kill me, often warning me that she would do it while I was asleep. I had trouble sleeping because of her threats, so I would usually push my heavy dresser against my bedroom door in an attempt to keep her out while I slept. Thus far, she had never actually attempted to kill me, but I did not trust her. She would do things to leave me confused and frightened such as telling me she had poisoned my food and then threatening to harm me if I did not eat it. Knowing what bizarre things she was capable of, I quickly learned not to trust anything—not only the words that she said, but also the words that anybody else said.

As I sat in the car feeling anxious about what could happen with my family, my hand touched the little Bible in my pocket. I took it out and flipped through small gold edged pages. I looked at some of the words, but it seemed confusing. I did not understand what I was reading. I turned to the first page and read the very first line. *"In the beginning, God created the heavens and the earth."* Genesis 1:1.

I paused to ponder that. Somewhere in my past, I had heard that the creation of the earth began as the result of a huge explosion that created everything. I struggled now to make sense of that. If there ever were a time that absolutely nothing existed, then there would still be nothing. That meant there had to be something that always existed. What was that something? Perhaps a single cell? No, something else would have had to create that cell. I looked again at the passage I had read. It appeared it was saying that God existed in the beginning. It was at that moment that I chose to believe that God indeed did exist. It made far more sense to me that a supreme being had created the earth rather than nothing suddenly erupting into something. It set right with me that God was real. However, if everything had to have a beginning, then who or what created God? Perhaps I could find that answer if I read further.

I read the first four chapters of Genesis carefully while I sat in the car. I did not find an answer about who created God, but I did find it compelling as I read about how God had created the first human beings and how the devil had convinced those humans to disobey God. Because the humans had disobeyed Him, God drove them out of the garden in which they were living. It was at that point that I developed the view that God must be a mean and unyielding God who was difficult to please and quick to punish. He had severely punished the first humans for their very first mistake. The mistake happened to be eating fruit from a particular tree after He had told them not to eat it. It did not seem like that big of a deal to me. *He must be a mean God if He would punish people for eating fruit,* I thought. I would not want a God like that, who expected perfection from people. If He had become so angry with people just for eating some fruit, who knows what He would do if somebody did something *really* wrong.

"Ginny!" My thoughts about God were interrupted by the sound of my father hollering. He had stood up and was pounding on the front door. "Open this door before I bust it in and then I'll bust your head in along with it!"

My mother was not afraid of anybody, least of all my father, so I was surprised when she opened the door and let him into the house. I shoved the Bible back into my pocket and hurried out of the car to follow him before my mother could lock the door again. There would be time to think about God later. For now, it was time to go back to trying to survive in my dysfunctional family.

~

Having a job meant the world to me; I threw myself into caring for the residents, but it was difficult for me with my emotional symptoms. Chronic depression left me feeling exhausted most of the time, compounded by the constant anxiety I had over my home life. It was difficult to concentrate at work when I was worried about what I would find once I returned home. The dread that I felt would make it hard for me to function at work, but I held onto that job for dear life. It was the only positive thing that I had in my life.

I was great when it came to patient care, but I avoided interactions with the staff as much as possible. I was not good at fostering any relationships because I felt that they required too much effort. My social skills were lacking, and I was awkward around everybody. I never knew how to act or what to say, so I kept to myself as much as I could and spoke to the staff only when necessary. I overheard some of them making comments about me being strange, but I had such strong work ethics and cared so well for the residents that they left me alone. Everyone that is, except for Gloria.

Gloria did not work on the same floor that I did, so I found it odd that I kept running into her. I tried avoiding her, and I even tried being rude to her, but her interest in me did not wane. I felt bothered by her attention. It made me feel tired. Whenever I saw her coming, I would try to hide. I had been working at the nursing home for three weeks and was on my way home one day when she saw me in the parking lot. She ran up to me before I could get my car unlocked and get safely inside. "Where are you going right now?" she asked.

"Home," I said.

"Are you hungry?" Gloria asked. "I've got some free time right now, and I'm famished. Would you like to stop somewhere and get something to eat with me? My treat."

I never went to restaurants with other people because I felt so self-conscious about eating in front of them. It was an awkward situation for me. "I need to get home," I said. "I have some business to take care of." The only business I had was to go to bed and pull the covers over my head, but she did not need to know that.

"Come with me," Gloria said. "I won't keep you more than an hour. I promise."

"Why can't you leave me alone?" I snapped. "Can't you see me trying to avoid you?" I felt guilty for being rude to her, but at that moment, my self-preservation was more important than her feelings.

"Of course, I know you are trying to avoid me," Gloria replied, "but I don't give up when God places somebody on my heart."

"Not that again," I said. "I told you I decided there must be a God. What more do you want from me?"

"I'd like you to know God," Gloria said. "He wants to know you."

I scoffed at that. "I looked through the Bible you gave me," I said. "I'm not interested in knowing a mean God like that. I already have enough mean people in my life. Thanks, but no thanks."

Gloria looked surprised. "What makes you think God is mean?" she asked.

"The proof is in the pudding," I replied. "God threw Adam and Eve out of the garden just because they ate some fruit. Then there was all that stuff about sin offerings and guilt offerings. Then all those rules and laws He made. From the little bit that I did look at, all I saw was God demanding perfection from people. That is too much for me to deal with. Some of those rules He made sounded ridiculous. He even says to stone people to death if they do not obey those ridiculous rules. What kind of God is that?" I caught myself feeling angry. I wondered why I cared enough about it to feel angry.

I saw amusement dance in Gloria's eyes. "Lisa, you did not understand what you were reading," she said.

"What is so difficult to understand about words printed in black and white?" I said. "I know how to read."

Gloria glanced at her watch. "Let's not talk about it here in the parking lot," she said. "Come have something to eat with me. I would like to help you know God."

"I am not interested," I said.

"God loves you, Lisa. He loves you very much. He wants you to know Him," Gloria said.

I stopped short. Love was a word that made me feel uncomfortable. I did not know much about love. Why would God love me when even my parents could not? I was not worthy of love. How could Gloria possibly know that God loved me when God and I did not know each other? "I am tired," I said wearily, dragging the back of my hand across my eyes.

"Just give me one hour," Gloria pleaded.

I hesitated. It was hard for me to admit to myself that I was interested in the mean God who supposedly loved me. I decided I would give Gloria an hour. Her pursuance of me was wearing on me. Maybe if I listened to her talk about God for an hour, she would leave me alone after that. As tired as I was, I was glad to delay going home for a little while longer.

The restaurant that Gloria took me to was a small quiet place near the nursing home. We sat in a corner booth, and I made sure my back was to the rest of the patrons. I ordered a hamburger and then sat there fingering my napkin as an awkward silence lingered between us. After the food arrived, Gloria finally started talking. I listened quietly as she explained to me that the Bible is written in two sections. The Old Testament is about God dealing with His chosen people from Israel called the Israelites. The New Testament is all about Jesus, who she explained is God's son, whom God had sent from heaven to earth as a baby to die a gruesome death in place of humans so that humans could find favor with God.

When I expressed confusion about it, Gloria explained in more detail. "When Adam and Eve disobeyed God by eating that fruit, it brought sin into the world," she said. "God cannot tolerate sin. In the Old Testament times, people had to sacrifice animals to atone for their sins. The blood of the animals saved the people from God's wrath. However, God had a better plan for saving people than animal sacrifices. One day He sent His only son, Jesus, to earth so that Jesus could die for all the people who have sinned. The blood of Jesus took the place of the former animal sacrifices.

Now, God has made it so that all people must do if they desire to be saved is to accept Jesus as their Savior and repent of their sins. If you do that, will be saved. That means you will become restored in God's eyes, and after you die, you will live with Him forever."

I did not see any love in God allowing His son to die as some sacrifice to please Him. It only reiterated that God was mean.

The voices rose into my mind immediately. *I think I like God,* I heard. *I hope she tells us more about Him.*

A light came on in my mind. "I saw on television Jesus beaten and then crucified on a cross," I remembered. "I did not understand it."

"That was Jesus sacrificing Himself for you and me and everybody," Gloria said. "He died the death that we deserve because we are sinners. If we believe that Jesus died in our place and confessed Him as our Savior, then our sins are wiped clean, and we become restored in God's eyes. That is what the New Testament section of the Bible is all about. It tells all about Jesus and His life and death. It also tells how the first Christians and the early church got started."

I found Gloria's words fascinating. I believed her story about Jesus. I had no doubt that it was true, and I felt touched that Jesus would endure such a death for people who deserved it, but I did not deserve it. "I don't think He died for me," I said. "My mother tells me that I am worthless, but I do not think I am a sinner. I've never committed a crime or anything bad like that."

Gloria's eyes were soft and her voice gentle. "Lisa, every single person that has ever lived is a sinner," she said. "The Bible says that we all fall short to God. It also says that if we say we have no sin, we deceive ourselves. Committing crimes is not the only thing that deems you as a sinner. Even smaller things like lying and complaining are sins. God is so holy that He cannot tolerate even the smallest sin. All sins are equal to God. That means telling a lie is the same as murdering a person as far as God is concerned. That is why every single person needs a savior. That is why God sent His son to be our Savior and to take the punishment that we deserve. God loves people so much that He sent His son to die in our place."

"If Jesus died in our place then why do people still die?" I asked. "If He died for us then why don't people live forever?"

"People do live forever," Gloria said. "Once you are born you will always exist. God has appointed people to die a physical death, but after death, you will still be conscious. If you accepted Jesus as your Savior, you would reside with God forever. If you do not accept Jesus, you will be separated from God forever and reside in hell."

I nearly choked on my burger. "That is what I am saying about God being mean," I said. "Why would a loving God send anybody to hell just because that person did not accept Jesus as their Savior? God sounds very rigid and demanding."

Gloria's words about God and His plan for human salvation upset me. As if it were not enough that I was already worthless and ugly, now I could also add sinner to my list. It seemed like everywhere I turned I was being told how bad I was, first by my mother and now by God. Even if Jesus did die for me, I felt too worthless to accept it. I felt a heavy sense of burden on my shoulders that Jesus had paid such a price for the likes of me. God's plan of salvation only left me feeling more depressed. I could not measure up to God's standards. I believed that He would expect perfection from me and especially if I became saved. I knew I would only fail.

Gloria then asked me if I wanted to pray to God and accept Jesus as my Savior right then. Apparently, God was a spirit that you could talk to anywhere at any time. I could talk to God out loud or even in my head, and He would always hear me. Something in me desired to say yes. The voices in my head were like a cheering section, encouraging me to accept Jesus. I wanted to accept Him and become restored in God's eyes, but not only was I afraid of failing God, but I also thought that being saved meant I would have to become one of those fanatical holy rollers that so many people dreaded having contact with. When I finally responded to Gloria, I told her that I needed time to think about it. Becoming saved would probably put pressures and expectations on me that I could not handle. I just did not have the energy to live up to God's demanding and strict standards.

Gloria seemed disappointed, but she remained cheerful. Quietly I listened while she chattered on about how much God loves people and how He can help with any problem and bring peace and joy into my life. I had a harder time believing in having peace and joy in my life than I did believing in Jesus. "All you have to do is ask Him for help," she said. "God will never fail you. He will never let you down."

I finished my burger and looked at my watch. I felt more tired than ever. I think Gloria expected me to show excitement over all she had just told me about God and Jesus. While I believed what she had told me, it did not make a huge impact on me. I still had the same dysfunctional life. She had given me knowledge about God, but I had no emotions about it. "You promised me one hour," I said. "That hour is up."

Once I was home, I locked myself in my bedroom and thought about all that Gloria had told me. I could hear my parents screaming at each other, so I decided to put my newfound information to the test. "God, if you are real, please make my parents stop fighting so I can have quiet tonight," I prayed.

I waited. Gloria said God would help me with anything if I asked Him. My parents kept screaming. Thinking maybe God was busy and had not heard me, I repeated my request.

Maybe my request was too difficult for God. I opened up my bedroom window and said, "God, if you are real, prove it to me. Make the wind blow right now." However, there was no wind.

I spent the next ten minutes asking God to prove Himself. Surely, He would not mind proving to me that He was real. If He could create the entire world, then the little tricks that I wanted Him to do should not be too difficult for Him.

God did not respond to any of my tests. I was sorely disappointed. How did God expect me to believe anything about Him unless He proved Himself to me first? I picked up the Bible Gloria had given me and began to leaf through it. I flipped around in it and read a few scriptures here and there. I felt my frustration mounting. I chose to believe that God was real;

now He should give me a sign to reward my new belief. I felt entitled to that much from Him.

I was about to give up on it and close the book when my eyes landed on Matthew 16:4: *"Only a wicked and adulterous generation would demand a miraculous sign, but the only sign I will give them the sign of the prophet Jonah."* I felt my cheeks burning with shame. I did not know who the prophet Jonah was, but I sure knew what God thought about people asking Him for signs to prove His identity. Had God just spoken to me through those words in that Bible? I had not heard an audible voice, but I felt as though He had spoken to me. It made me think that I wanted to read more of the Bible see what other answers to my many questions I might find in there.

I ignored my clamoring exhaustion as I settled into bed to read. I quickly gave up on trying reading anything in the Old Testament. It was too confusing to me. I could understand everything up to Genesis chapter 4, but beyond that, I was lost. To me, it was just a dry book about who begat who and God making laws and rules that seemed impossible to follow. I turned to the New Testament and started there. It was much easier to understand. It was not long before I was reading eagerly. I was fascinated to learn about Jesus, the son of God who had come to earth to talk about God and love and peace. He was so gentle and good, and He went around with his 12 followers preaching good messages. I felt so moved by Jesus that my eyes filled with tears when I came to the part about Him being beaten and crucified. It appalled me that people would do that to such a kind and gentle person. I thought about how Jesus must have loved people if He was willing to go to that level of torture for them.

I was still thinking about Jesus when my door flew open, and my mother stormed into my room. She looked furious and my stomach instantly formed a knot. I had no idea why she was so angry. I could tell by her glassy eyes that she was drunk or that she had been abusing her pain medication again. "Didn't you hear me calling you?" she demanded.

"I was reading," I said. "I did not hear you."

"Reading what?" she yelled. She tore the book out of my hand and looked at it. "You are reading the Bible?" She said in an incredulous voice. "Do you think the Bible is going to help you?" She laughed and tossed it casually to the floor.

I rushed to pick it up. It bothered me that my mother had thrown a book about Jesus on the floor like that. I had just read about Jesus' crucifixion, and it seemed disrespectful to toss His story onto the floor.

"I want you to come downstairs and clean up the mess down there," my mother said. She was swaying back and forth because she could barely keep herself upright.

I wanted to scream at her; *you trashed the house, now you clean your mess!* I knew if I dared to stand up to her, I would be sleeping outside that night. Hatred filled my heart like a festering boil. Just once, I wanted to tell her exactly what I thought of her. However, even though I despised her and wished her dead, she was still my mother. I had no respect for her personally, but I did respect her position in my life.

I placed the Bible on my dresser and followed my mother downstairs. When I saw the extent of the mess, I nearly fainted. It would probably take me half the night to clean up that mess, and I was already exhausted. Without a word, I began to pick up shards of broken glass and beer cans.

"She was up there reading the Bible," my mother said to my father. He was sitting on the couch in a torn T-shirt. I assumed my mother had cut up all of his clothes again.

"The Bible?" My father snorted. I had no regard for my father either. I did not hate him; I just had no relationship with him. He never had much to do with my brothers or me.

"That's what I said," my mother replied sarcastically.

I do not know how long it took me to clean up their mess, but it felt like hours. When I finished, I went back up to my room. I felt defeated. If I did not get away from my family soon, I knew I would be heading for a third suicide attempt. I was lost, and I had no chance of finding myself unless I got out of there. I saw the Bible sitting on my dresser. Gloria had said that God could help me with any problem.

I did not want to ask God because I still thought of Him as mean, but I saw Jesus in a completely different light. Maybe Jesus could help me. "Jesus, I accept you as my Savior," I said quietly. "I need help, and I do not have anywhere else to turn. I do not know if you can help me, but I need to get out of here. I am never going to make it if I do not get free from here. I am broken. I am lost, and I feel crazy. I have no hope. I don't even have my sanity." My voice trembled, and I wiped tears from my eyes. "You are my last resort. I know it is such a long shot. I make minimum wage, and there is no way I can afford a place of my own. I do not have a penny in savings. I do not have anything at all. I have no money to buy what I would need. I feel trapped in a hopeless situation. I know you worked many miracles in the Bible. I will go to the store tomorrow and buy a lottery ticket. I will know if you want to help me because I will win enough money to get my own place and buy everything that I need."

Some say when you are saved you become a different person, but I did not feel any different. Even after I professed Jesus as my Savior, I still felt hopeless and depressed. I was disappointed that I did not feel an immediate life change. However, I did have a little hope that my prayer for help in getting away from my family might bear fruit. I knew the answer that I wanted, and I told Jesus as much in case He was not able to figure out the answer Himself. Winning the lottery was the only answer.

On my way to work the next morning, I stopped at the gas station and bought a few of the instant win lottery tickets. My heart thumped in anticipation as I feverishly scratched at the tickets. The first two were losers. The third one yielded me a win of one dollar. I was not about to give up. If Jesus had performed all of those miracles in the Bible, He could surely make me into a big lottery winner. I went back to the gas station and used the winning dollar ticket to purchase another ticket. It was another loser.

I put my head on the steering wheel and fought back the tears. I had prayed to Jesus and had even given Him the easy answer to my prayer. Gloria was wrong. My first prayer to Jesus and He had let me down in a big way. I could not depend on people, and now it seemed that I could not depend on Jesus either.

I stopped thinking about my disappointment with Jesus as I made my way to work. The next time I ran into Gloria, I had a thing or two to say to her about her faith in answered prayer!

A few minutes before I was due to go home, the Director of Nursing stopped me and thrust a piece of paper toward me. "Would you be so kind as to hang this note up on the bulletin board at the time clock on your way out?" she asked.

I took the paper from her. After she had walked away, I glanced at it. It said, "Apartment for rent behind nursing home. See Administrator for details."

Instead of hanging that note at the time clock, I went directly to the Administrator's office. I was not sure what compelled me to go there. I knew there was no way I could afford an apartment with the money that I was making. I was going to look like a fool to inquire about it.

I had never spoken to the Administrator. He was a big burly man who looked intimidating. Nervously I tried to look him in the eyes as I handed the paper to him.

"Are you interested in the apartment?" he asked.

I could not find my voice, so I simply nodded.

The Administrator looked at me over the top of his glasses. "The company that owns this building also owns the big house behind it," he said. "The house is split into three apartments. We rent out those apartments to our employees. The second-floor apartment recently became available. Do you have a family?"

I shook my head. "It would just be me," I said. I could hear my voice shaking. "What is the monthly rent?"

"Well, I'll tell you what." He shuffled some papers around on his desk. "I need some real help over there. I just kicked the tenants out. They trashed the apartment, and it needs work. Trash needs picking up, and all the walls need painting. The appliances need cleaning. If the next person who rents it is willing to do that work, I will rent it to that person at a low cost. Two fifty a month and the tenant would be responsible for their electric bill."

I could hardly believe my ears. Renting an apartment for just two hundred and fifty dollars a month? That would be within my price range. I could barely contain my excitement as I said loudly, "I will take it! I will do all of the work!"

"You have not seen it," he warned. "You might not want it after you see what a mess it is."

"I don't care how much of a mess it is," I said. "I need a place to live."

"You better look at it first," he said. "I will have the maintenance supervisor take you over there."

I fell in love with the apartment the minute I saw it. It was huge, with two bedrooms, a living room, kitchen, and even a small dining room. I could not believe that I was going to have such a large beautiful apartment for just two hundred and fifty dollars a month. I had to pinch myself to prove to myself that I was not dreaming. It was finally happening. I had a real chance of getting away from my family and getting on my own. It did not matter to me how much work needed to be done to get it into live in shape. I was willing to work my fingers to the bone to call that apartment my own. I could not wait to be away from my family and to try to straighten myself out and make a life for myself.

I realized then that Jesus had answered my prayer. My first prayer answered in a mighty way! He had not answered it the way that I expected him to. Winning the lottery would have made everything much easier but getting that trashed up apartment for such a low monthly rent was even better than winning the lottery. Not only was I excited about having a place of my own, but I was also thrilled that my prayer was answered.

# Five

*The righteous cry out, and the Lord hears, and delivers them out of all their troubles. (Psalm 34:17)*

My mother did not take the news that I was moving out well. She was furious that she was losing control over me. She forbade me to leave, but she knew that at my age she could not stop me. Since she could not prevent me from going, she did the only thing that she could do, which was to refuse to allow me to take anything with me that I had not paid for myself: including my bed, dresser, and most of my clothing. I moved into my apartment with nothing other than the few meager possessions that I owned— a few clothes and the bible that Gloria had given me.

The first few nights in my new apartment, I slept on the floor because I had no bed or furniture of any kind. I slept with great peace for the first time in my life, knowing that I no longer had to fear the possibility of my mother harming me or listen to the sounds of screaming and violence.

While I was thrilled to escape my dysfunctional family life, having my apartment brought its own set of challenges. Once on my own, the symptoms of my mental illness quickly worsened. I began having blackouts more frequently and would often wake up to find myself in unfamiliar places. Soon it seemed that the only time I was in a fully conscious state was when I had to work. I was running on empty when at work. Despite being in an altered state of consciousness so much of the time, I felt like I never slept. It was difficult to function while working with such chronic exhaustion.

Random items began appearing in my apartment that I did not remember purchasing. I was used to finding children's items, but I was shocked when bigger things started showing up on my doorstep that I knew I did not have the money to buy. By the time I realized that a credit card had been obtained in my name, I was already over one thousand dollars in debt. When I examined the credit card application, I found it had been made out in my name, but the form was not my handwriting.

One morning, I woke up to find that my second bedroom was turned into a child's bedroom without my knowledge. I decided that I could not take any more of my life. I had spent a lifetime trying to hide my secrets from other people, but I broke down and shared some details about my life with Gloria. She worked on the psychiatric floor at the nursing home, and I thought that she could tell me some ways of dealing with my schizophrenia symptoms.

Gloria was surprised when I shared my symptoms with her. I took her to my second bedroom and allowed her to see what had become of it. She stood in the doorway and looked around the room with disbelief.

"Please do not tell anybody about this," I said. I was ashamed, and I wondered if I had made a mistake by sharing it with her.

Gloria turned to face me. "Lisa, I have worked with people who have schizophrenia for over twenty years," she said. "I have never heard of the symptoms that you are describing to me as those of schizophrenia. Even the type of voices you hear and the hallucinations that you have do not seem to match what the known ones are for schizophrenia."

"A psychiatrist diagnosed me," I said.

Gloria shook her head. "I think there is a reason that your medication is not decreasing your symptoms," she said. "I am not convinced that you have schizophrenia."

"Then what else could be wrong with me?" I asked in a trembling voice. "Do you think I could have something worse than schizophrenia?"

"I don't know," Gloria admitted. "I think you should go to another psychiatrist and get a second opinion. Because this—" she waved her hand inside the bedroom—"is not what is typically seen in schizophrenia."

I nearly broke down in tears of hysteria. If Gloria was correct, it meant that I was taking medication for the wrong condition.

"I am not a professional," Gloria went on. "Let's pray about it."

"What does God know about what is wrong with me?" I asked angrily.

"I know that you are a new Christian, so you don't know much about God yet," Gloria replied. "However, God is the only one who does know what you are dealing with right now. Let's pray that He will give another doctor the wisdom to figure out what is going on with you."

After she finished praying for me, Gloria began to put pressure on me to make an appointment with a new psychiatrist. I did not have much hope that another doctor would diagnose me with anything other than schizophrenia, but I relented under Gloria's persuasion and decided to get a second opinion. If nothing else, perhaps another doctor could prescribe a different medication that would work better for me.

~

Two months later, I was sitting in front of Dr. Thomas, a relatively young psychiatrist who had been seeing me twice a week for the previous eight weeks. After a thorough assessment of my symptoms and a detailed history of my medical history, he was ready to give me his diagnosis. Along with Dr. Thomas, I had also been seeing a new therapist who worked in conjunction with him. She was also there to agree with whatever he was about to tell me.

I was not expecting anything other than what I had already heard for two years, so it came as a surprise to me when Dr. Thomas told me he felt I had multiple issues. "The way that your mood alternates from periods of depression to periods of highs indicates that you have Bipolar Disorder," he said. "And based on your disjointed sense of self, problems with interpersonal relationships, self-harm behaviors and impulsivity, it appears that you also have a condition known as Borderline Personality Disorder."

"That sounds better than having schizophrenia," I said tiredly.

Dr. Thomas frowned at me. "Lisa, those are both serious mental illnesses that can cause marked impairments in your ability to function," he said.

"But at least I'm not schizophrenic, right?" I asked.

Out of the corner of my eye, I could see my therapist clasp her hands together and place them in her lap.

Dr. Thomas hesitated and cleared his throat before responding. "You do not have schizophrenia," he agreed slowly. "However, I am giving you another diagnosis, a quite rare condition that can appear very similar to schizophrenia."

I felt my heart sink. A third diagnosis? It just proved what a lost cause I was. There was no hope for me. "What is it?" I asked.

Dr. Thomas cleared his throat again and looked over at my therapist for confirmation. He seemed to be very deliberate and cautious in what he was saying to me.

"Well?" I shouted. "What is it?" I was struggling to control myself and not run screaming out of his office. His hesitation to tell me was frightening.

"Based on your symptoms and other criteria that your therapist and I have carefully studied –"

I jumped out of the chair so quickly that it toppled over behind me. I turned to my therapist, who was looking at me sympathetically. "Quit beating around the bush and tell me what is wrong with me!" I shouted.

"Lisa, you have Multiple Personality Disorder," my therapist blurted out.

A thick silence ensued as I struggled to comprehend what she said. I picked up my chair and sat back down. "What does that mean?" I asked.

After another moment of silence, my therapist tried to explain it to me. "You have altered aspects of your personality that manifest themselves as other people," she said.

"Tell me that in English," I said.

"Have you ever seen that movie called 'Sybil' starring Sally Field?" Dr. Thomas asked.

The movie sounded vaguely familiar to me. I remembered seeing parts of it when I was a teenager. I stared at my therapist with amazement. "Are you telling me that I walk around with other people in my body?" I asked.

My therapist struggled to explain it to me. "They are not real human beings," she said. "Technically they are all parts of you. They are all parts of your personality. They are people that you have created. When you think that you have lost consciousness, another aspect of your personality has taken control of your body and is functioning for you."

"Taking over my body?" I repeated. "It sounds as though aliens have invaded my body."

"These aspects of your personality have their own unique names," my therapist continued. "Some of them are children."

I stopped listening to her as an onslaught of memories rapidly flashed through my mind. I saw the toys, the purchases that I did not make, and the behaviors that I did not remember doing. I began to feel sick to my stomach. "You are wrong," I said. "This is all wrong. I have schizophrenia."

"No, Lisa," my therapist said. "I have met some of your alters. They have talked to me in my office. They made themselves known to me to help you from getting another wrong diagnosis. They don't want you given any more medication that would only harm you with severe side effects." She paused and lowered her voice. "They care for you, and they want to help you," she said quietly. "This disorder is rare, and it's usually found in people who have extreme abuse or other trauma in their childhoods. It is a disorder of survival."

I was too flabbergasted to say any more. The thought of walking around with assumed identities and especially as children was humiliating. I closed my eyes and envisioned a body my size sucking its thumb and playing with toys. The thoughts caused a shudder to pass through my body.

"Lisa, you are intelligent enough to understand and to deal with your disorder," my therapist said gently.

I looked at Dr. Thomas. "Is there a medication available that can cure this?" I asked.

Dr. Thomas shook his head. "I'm afraid there isn't," he said. "Treatment consists of psychotherapy with a therapist, and sometimes it can take years."

"Years?" I choked. I turned back to my therapist. "Do you know how to treat this disorder?" I asked her.

"It is rare enough that I have never come across it," my therapist admitted. "If you are willing to stick with me, we can learn how to treat it together."

"Like a guinea pig?" I asked sarcastically. 'I'm done with this for today. I am leaving."

My therapist looked concerned. "Will you be safe?" she asked.

"Is it these other people in my body who keep saving me?" I asked in return.

"Yes," my therapist replied.

"Why?" I railed. "If they can see that I do not want to live anymore, why do they keep trying to save my life?"

"They say there is a little part of you that wants to live and has hope that your life will somehow get better," my therapist said. "Now that you are away from your family, they see that chance that your life can improve, and you can find some peace."

I had heard enough. Feeling angry at the world, I stood up and stormed my way out of the office. When I got to my car, I realized that it was a rare moment that the voices in my head were quiet. I kicked my car tire and yelled, "Where are you now? Show yourselves, you cowards!" Then I burst into tears and collapsed to my knees. I did not care who saw me. I leaned against my car and sobbed. What was I going to do with three mental illnesses?

*Get up off the ground. Do not be so weak.*

I covered my ears with my hands and struggled to stand. My tears spent, I climbed into my car and drove. I was not going anywhere in particular except where the road would take me. Eventually, I stopped in front of a railroad crossing about three miles from my apartment. *Jesus, you promised peace to those who believe in you,* I sobbed. *You promised a sound mind. I have three mental illnesses. Does that sound like a sound mind to you?*

I decided right then that I was not going to endure any more years of psychiatric treatments and medications with their troublesome side effects. I had enough of it. I got out of my car, walked over to the railroad tracks, and laid my body on them. I laid on my back and looked up at the sky while I waited for a train to come along. If Jesus could speak to me, I could have used a few words from Him right then, but the only sound I heard was the agony of anguish in my mind. I knew there was no way this attempt would fail. I was going to find out for myself how bad of a sin suicide was.

As I lay there waiting for a train to end my life, a scripture from the Old Testament came to my mind. It was Isaiah 41:10. *Fear not, for I am with you; be not dismayed, for I am your God. I will strengthen you, yes, I will help you; I will uphold you with my righteous right hand.* I was surprised that I could remember that scripture because I had read very little of the Old Testament. *Is Jesus speaking to me through that scripture?* I wondered. *Is He here with me while I wait for a train to snuff out my life?*

This time I could not fail. I would never survive being run over by a train.

"Get up, Lisa," I heard a voice say. "You know that we are not going to let you get hit by a train."

I sat up on the track and looked around. Next to me stood a young woman with long black hair and deep green eyes. She appeared older than the dark-haired child that I usually saw. I reached out to touch her, but when I did, I could not feel her. I saw my hand resting on her leg, but I was touching nothing but air. I felt frightened because I was not sure if I had a complete psychotic breakdown and was no longer operating in reality.

# Six

*I will not leave you orphans; I will come to you.*
*(John 14:18)*

"Don't be frightened," the woman said gently. "I am not going to hurt you, but I do wish you would get off of these train tracks before we have to take control and get you off of them."

I reached out and picked up one of the rocks that were on the side of the tracks. I could feel the rock in the palm of my hand. I let it fall back to the ground and touched the person standing next to me again. I still could not feel her. "Are you real?" I asked.

"To you, I am real," the woman said. "Please get off of the tracks so that I can properly introduce myself."

I looked down the tracks to see if a train was approaching. "I want to die," I said.

"You are not going to die today," the woman said. "I am sorry to do this to you, but you are not giving me a choice. Mouse, can you get Lisa off the tracks?"

On the left side of me, another person suddenly appeared. She also looked young and had long blonde hair that framed her face as she leaned over to peer at me. I was beyond flabbergasted as I looked back into her face. "Where did you come from?" I asked.

The girl ignored me. "I will get Lisa off of the tracks if I can have an extra treat today," she said to the woman on my right.

"Really, Mouse." The woman sounded exasperated. "Why is it that you cannot be helpful unless you get treats? I have told you how selfish that is."

"I am not selfish. Treats make life more fun," Mouse said.

"Okay. If you get Lisa off these tracks, I will make sure you get another treat today."

"It's a deal," Mouse replied excitedly, and then she disappeared as quickly as she had arrived. A few seconds later, I felt my body being moved back into a standing position and walking to my car.

I sat in my car and tried to process what had just happened to me. I had just become co-conscious with two of my alters, and they had controlled my body without me losing consciousness. My fright disappeared and was replaced with a sense of confusion and disorientation. I felt like I had taken several sleeping pills and was not being allowed to go to sleep.

The long black-haired woman was still visible next to me. "How many times do we have to save you before you finally understand we are not going to let you die?" she asked me. "You can be as frustrating to me as Mouse can be." She shook her head.

"Where did the other one go?" I asked. "The one that you called Mouse… where did she go? I do not see her now."

"She is here inside of your head," the woman said. "If you concentrate hard enough, you will see all of us."

I took a deep breath. "I do not want to see anybody else," I said. "What is your name?"

"Everybody in here calls me Little One. You can call me that too."

"You don't look little," I said.

"We do not have ages as you do," Little One said. "I used to be little, but I have changed. You are the one who changed me from being little into being more mature. But everybody is used to calling me Little One, so we decided to stick with that name."

The loud blast of a train horn caused me to jump in my seat. A long train decorated with painted graffiti roared past my car.

"It's a good thing we were not on the tracks," a third voice said. "Our body would have been all mushed up."

"Bug, that is enough with the gloomy talk," Little One said.

"What kind of names are Bug and Mouse?" I asked.

"They do not have names. They go by nicknames," Little One explained.

"They are the ones who draw the pictures I find hanging up in my apartment," I said.

"True," Little One agreed. "Speaking of apartments, why don't you take us home to a safe place where we can get to know each other better?"

I grasped the steering wheel and shook my head. "I do not want to know any of you people. I want you to leave," I said. "Get out of my body or out of my mind, wherever you are."

"It does not work that way," Little One said. "You have created us to help you survive your life."

"No," I denied. "That cannot be true. I never wanted to survive my life."

I felt a surge of anger rise from somewhere inside of me. "Let Lisa return to the tracks if she does not appreciate us," a high-pitched voice piped up. The voice spoke so rapidly that I had a difficult time making out the words.

"Another one?" I gasped. "Who was that?"

"That was Little Lisa," Little One said.

I began to beat my hands on the steering wheel with frustration. I could not keep track of the different names and voices. "How many of you are there?" I cried out.

"There have been many of us," Little One replied calmly. "Right now, there are just four of us. There is me, Mouse, Bug and Little Lisa."

"Why does she have my name?" I asked. "I do not want any of you to share my name."

"Listen here." The high-pitched voice sounded indignant. "I am not exactly proud to carry your name. You are not my favorite person here. You are only good for causing me a headache."

"Little Lisa!" Little One admonished. "That was mean. How can you talk to Lisa in that manner? She is the very one who brought you into existence."

"I don't care," Little Lisa snapped. "If she does not appreciate all that we have done for her, she can go back and lay on the tracks for all I care."

Little One seemed embarrassed. "I apologize for Little Lisa's outburst," she said. "She is not very good at hiding her feelings."

"Why should I hide them?" Little Lisa asked blandly. "Lisa has been hiding her feelings all of her life and look where it has gotten her. She is now a nut job."

My shock over meeting some of my alters began to give way to annoyance with Little Lisa. I disliked her immediately. She was brash and outspoken, and not very kind.

Little Lisa sensed my dislike toward her. "You do not like me?" She laughed. "You are the one who made me everything that I am. Little One can coddle you if she wants to, but do not expect me to tiptoe through the tulips with you. I think you are a dumb ass. You should face the consequences of your behaviors. If you want to get run over by a train that is your decision."

"But then you will be a murderer," Bug spoke up. "If you kill yourself, you will kill us too. Then you will be wanted by the FBI, and your picture will be on posters all over town."

I had enough. I climbed out of the car and stormed back to the railroad tracks. I stood next to them and looked both ways for an oncoming train. "I am getting away from you people," I said angrily. "I am not living like this."

"Murderer!" Bug yelled. "Serial killer! Wanted by the FBI."

"That is enough," Little One said in a warning tone.

"Why doesn't Lisa like us?" Bug asked. "I thought she would like to be with us."

"She just has to get used to us," Little One replied. "It may be difficult for her to adjust to sharing her body with us."

My heart quickened, and my desperation rose as I frantically wished for a train to take me away from what was happening to me. I could not

live like this. I would have preferred to continue having blackouts rather than to meet the people who were sharing space in my mind.

"I am bored with this game now," Little Lisa said. "Let's go home."

"You have no home," I told her hotly. "I have an apartment in which you do not belong. None of you is welcome there. There is only one name on the lease, and that is mine."

"Now we are going to be homeless," Bug cried. "We are going to be dead and homeless."

"If it were not for us helping you function you would not have a job or an apartment," Little Lisa said, and her anger matched mine. "Without us, you would be living on the streets or in a mental institution. Take your pick."

My anger towards Little Lisa was growing more rageful by the second. I felt desperate to get away from her. A train could not come fast enough. More than I wanted to kill myself, I also wanted to kill her.

As I was looking down the tracks for a train, I suddenly felt my body spinning in circles. Mouse had taken control of my body, and she was spinning around with her arms outstretched. When she stopped, she hugged herself and looked up at the sky. "Life is good," she said brightly. "God lives above those clouds, and He is looking down at me."

I do not know what stunned me more— the fact that Mouse said life was good, or that she knew who God was.

"Little One, God says it is time for my extra treat," Mouse giggled.

"Oh, Mouse. You know God did not say that," Little One chided.

"He did too," Mouse insisted. "He said that since I saved Lisa's life again, I deserve my extra treat."

A gentle breeze blew a tuft of hair across my face. Taking control of the body from Mouse, I lifted my hand and brushed the hair away. Curiosity got the better of me, and I forgot about the train. "How do you know anything about God? I asked.

"I hear what you hear," Mouse replied. "I heard Gloria tell you about God and Jesus." She took control of my body back and wandered away from the tracks into the grass. "Besides, I have been to church."

I was surprised. "When did you go to church?" I asked.

"When you were little," Mouse said. "The next-door neighbor took us to Sunday school at her church a few times. It was great fun."

I struggled to remember going to church but only found a dark and empty spot in my mind where the memory would have been. "I do not know a thing about that," I said. "I don't know if I believe you. My mother would not have let me go anywhere with the neighbor, especially not to the church."

"Your mother was too drunk to know or to care where you were going," Mouse said. "I went a few times, but when your mother did find out, she stopped us from going anymore."

"Your mother is a witch," Little Lisa said.

I ignored that. "Why would you go to Sunday school instead of me going there?" I asked Mouse.

"Because it was fun," Mouse replied. "I am the one in here who likes to do fun things. You are always afraid to have fun. I liked Sunday school. One time while I was there, I made a cardboard cutout of Jesus." She paused and then pointed to the clouds. "Jesus is God's son," she added. "He is up there too."

"I know who Jesus is," I said quietly. I was still trying to digest the idea of Mouse having attended Sunday school in my place.

"Can you take me back to Sunday school?" Mouse asked.

I did not know how to respond to her, so I did not reply

"We no longer have a little body," Little One. "We cannot go to a Sunday school for children anymore now that we have an adult body. Lisa would have to go to an adult Bible study now."

"Shucks," Mouse said. "Sometimes I do not like this big body because it gets in the way of my fun." She bent down and picked the dandelion out of the grass. "God wants me to tell Lisa that she thinks the wrong way about Him," she said as she twirled the dandelion around in her fingers. "God wants you to know that He is not mean."

"God does not speak to you," I said. I felt uncomfortable that one of my alters might have more knowledge about God that I did. "God only speaks through the Bible these days."

"If that were true, He would not have told me to help you understand that He is not a mean God," Mouse said in a haughty tone.

"Do not put false words into God's mouth," I warned. "Anything He has to say to me will come from the Bible."

Mouse tossed the dandelion to the ground and put her hands on her hips. "He talked to me because you do not understand the Bible correctly," she said. "You read some of it, and now you think He is a mean and punishing God."

Before I could respond to that, Little Lisa pushed forth to make her obtrusive presence known. "God has more patience with you than I do," she said. "I am done with this. I am not going to stand out here all day while you wait to jump in front of a train. I am taking us home. You have met us, and even though you did not jump on the welcome wagon, I guess this could have gone much worse than it did."

"Lisa is smart enough to understand what is happening here," Little One remarked. "We have all been making our presence known to her for years."

I felt a huge lump in my throat. So much had happened to me during that last hour that I was still feeling shocked. I did not know where my life was going to go from that point or how I was going to adjust to my life being co-conscious with alters. Based on the many symptoms I had experienced over the years, it now made sense that I had Multiple Personality Disorder since childhood. Knowing that I had alters in my body was jarring enough for me but meeting four different alters with such drastically different personalities was more than overwhelming. I knew that I was going to have to utilize my therapist to help me understand why this disorder had happened to me, but I did not know if she could help me adjust to it and cope with it.

Little Lisa's chirping birdlike voice broke into my thoughts. "I am going home now," she said.

Nobody moved. My body stood rooted in one spot.

"Homeward bound," Little Lisa said. "That is where I am going."

Still, my body did not move. I had a sense that all four of them were looking at each other and waiting for something.

Little Lisa's tone of voice turned sheepish. "We need a little help here," she said. "Lisa, can you take us home? None of us know how to drive a car but you."

I felt my eyes narrow into slits. For all of Little Lisa's tough talk, she was now at my mercy, and it felt good.

"I will not beg you," Little Lisa said. "I will leave the car here, and I will walk all the way home before I beg you."

I sensed that Little Lisa was stubborn enough to leave my car there, so I was dismayed to realize that she had the upper hand. I did not want to leave my car there, so I relented and began walking toward it.

"It is the start of a new life," Mouse said happily, as I got back in the car. "You are finally going to see that life can be good."

I laughed bitterly as I started the car. "I hate life," I said sourly. "I have had a dysfunctional and abusive childhood, and now in my adult life I have alters and other mental disorders."

"Cry me a river," Little Lisa said. "Many people have it worse than you do."

"Do not deny me the right to feel sorry for myself!" I shouted. "There may be people who have life worse than I do, but I have had a life worse than many have had."

"Please, nobody disturb Lisa while she is driving," Little One said. "It could cause her to crash the car."

"Then we will be dead, and blowflies will leave maggots on our decaying body," Bug said matter-of-factly.

"God is the author of both life and death," Mouse said. "And He made me an author of life in here."

"We will see about that," I sighed.

"We will see," Mouse agreed. Suddenly she yelled, "Stop here!" and caused my foot to slam on the brakes so hard that the car screeched to a stop.

"Mouse, what in the world are you doing?" Little One asked.

Mouse giggled and pointed at the donut shop across the street. "The treat that I want is in that shop," she said. "It is hard work to be an author

of life in here. From now on, I need a treat every day. Treats make life fun."
She got out of the car and began to rummage through my pockets for
money. "God is finally going to make everything right in this life," she said
as she scampered across the street.

## Seven

*It shall come to pass that before they call, I will*
*answer; and while they are still speaking, I will*
*hear. (Isaiah 65:24)*

The day after I became co-conscious with my alters, I had a long appointment with my therapist. She was concerned that I would sink into a major depressive episode, but I was angrier than anything else. She explained details about Multiple Personality Disorder that I already knew from my research, particularly that I had created alters at different time periods during my childhood to help myself cope with the abuse and other traumas I had experienced within my dysfunctional family. She went on to explain that these alters were not real people who could function on their own. Every decision that they made, every action they took, and every word they spoke was somehow controlled unconsciously by me. I gave every ability they had to them. The concept that my strings controlled them like puppets was difficult for me to adjust to. I did not want to take responsibility for any of them.

"What you are saying is that Multiple Personality Disorder is an acting job," I told my therapist. "This is nothing more than me pretending to be other people."

"I would not view it in that manner," my therapist replied. "This disorder is a complicated phenomenon deeply rooted in trauma and intricately developed by an intelligent and creative mind."

"So, it is an acting job that could win me an Academy Award," I said sarcastically. "If I can control it, then I can end it."

"It doesn't work that way," my therapist warned. "This disorder requires long-term psychological treatment, and you also have the additional complications of other mental illnesses as well."

"If you are telling me that I am the master of this disorder then I can stop it," I insisted confidently. "I am going to step off from this stage and retire from this featured role."

"You are going to set yourself up for a major setback," my therapist said. "Instead of fighting against this disorder, you should be trying to learn how to cooperate with your alters to enhance your quality of life."

"Give me one week, and I will be cured," I said.

Seven days later, after a chaotic week of fighting against my alters and trying every way that I could think of to eliminate them, my therapist had me admitted into the psychiatric unit at a local hospital to keep me safe from self-harm behaviors. I was put into an empty room because the hospital staff feared that my having alters would be too disturbing for a roommate. Once in the hospital, I was placed on suicide watch, which meant that a staff member stayed with me around the clock to make sure that I did not attempt to injure myself.

Little Lisa was mortified that I had gotten us locked in a hospital and that a staff member watched us even during our most private moments, such as taking a shower and going to the bathroom. I was depressed, and the doctors tried switching my medications to alleviate my depression. The more depressed I became the angrier Little Lisa became with me.

Little One was relieved that I was in a place that would keep me safe. After eight days my psychiatrist felt that I was safe enough to be taken off suicide watch, and four days after that, I could return home with a rash of new medications in tow. My depression had lessened, but I felt utterly defeated that I had not been able to will my mental illnesses away. I knew that I was at a crossroads. I was going to have to keep trying to end my life, or I was going to have to accept that I was mentally ill and try to adjust to life with my disorders.

While Little One remained sympathetic toward me and tried to coddle me into having a more positive outlook, Little Lisa had zero patience for my episodes of depression or self-pity. She and I clashed frequently and had many arguments, with Little One trying to be the mediator between us. Many times, after Little Lisa and I would argue, Bug would become disturbed and attempt to run away. She would throw some of our clothes into a garbage bag and then wander around in the wooded area near my apartment. Bug was frightened by conflict of any kind and running away from it was always her answer to it. She was a weaker alter, and she never got very far before Little Lisa or Mouse would take control of the body and bring us back home.

I quickly learned that there were vast differences between these four alters. Little One and Little Lisa, although they both had the word 'little" in their names, were older personalities adept at helping me with my day to day functioning. Little One liked to do household tasks such as cleaning and laundry. Her favorite role was to have long talks with me to analyze my emotions and change my behaviors. She was fiercely loyal to me and protective of me to a fault. She did her best to make sure that everything was easy for me, and nothing aroused her anger more than my being hurt in any way. She often said that if it were possible, she would wrap me in bubble wrap and have me live alone in a locked room where nobody could hurt me. I grew to love her deeply because she worked so hard to keep me functioning as normally as I possibly could. She was my biggest cheerleader and spent hours encouraging me. She was always on alert and ready to help me with any troublesome issue that arose. Even when I was at my worst, Little One never gave up on me.

It was apparent that I had fashioned Little One out of my sense of responsibility. I had felt responsible for my brothers and my parents at an early age. At eight years old, I was worried about such things as the utilities being cut off at our house and where the next meal was going to come from. I had been forced into an adult role too early in life, and Little One was my response to that. I had formed her into being responsible and logical. Like me, she had difficulty enjoying anything or having fun. She was too worried about keeping life running as smoothly as possible.

"You're too stuffy," Mouse told Little One many times. "God wants us to have fun in life."

If Little One was too responsible, Mouse was anything but. She wanted nothing to do with responsibility or with anything that remotely resembled work. She insisted that life should be fun and free, and her biggest objective each day was to see how many treats she could obtain. She had a happy and positive disposition, and she was an expert at ignoring anything negative. She also tended toward lighthearted mischief that kept Little One on her toes.

I was uncomfortable with Mouse because I was not able to feel the joy or gratitude toward life that she did. I knew that her feelings about life came from somewhere deep within me, but I was not able to access those feelings. I had given up on joy and happiness at some point during my childhood and had siphoned those feelings over to Mouse. Joy and happiness were no longer safe feelings for me. In my world, those feelings were always accompanied by fear and loneliness. Consequently, seeing Mouse enjoy life caused me anxiety.

Mouse's enjoyment of life made me uneasy, but I admired both her ability to trust God and her lack of caring about what other people thought about her or her ideas. She had a strong and confident sense of self. Mouse seemed simple, but underneath her simplicity, she was intelligent and complex. Her simplicity was a ruse to avoid having to deal with any negativity. She did her best to ignore my troubled behaviors, and she refused to take sides in any argument.

While Mouse tried to display herself as simple, Bug more often showed her side of complexity. Although Bug was quiet and insecure, she was impeccably well-behaved and was often aghast at Mouse's shenanigans. Bug was a brooder who liked to stay to herself and ponder every situation. She seemed to be the alter most affected by the abuse and traumas that I had endured during my childhood. She loved God but was easily frightened and had difficulty with trust. I had molded her from my fears and insecurities. I felt a strong desire to love and protect Bug and to help that part of myself that was so raw and exposed to trauma and violence.

Of the four alters, I felt least connected to Little Lisa. She was flighty and hot-tempered. She had far less patience with my troubled behaviors and was quick to allow me to face the consequences of those behaviors. She was quick to become bored and had a flair for drama whenever she was upset. In therapy, I learned that Little Lisa was one of my core alters. She represented everything that I hated about myself. I saw Little Lisa as the part of me that my mother hated and that she had targeted for cruelty. I hated what Little Lisa represented to me—the worthless and ugly part of me that my mother wished was dead. I was unable to connect to any of Little Lisa's good qualities.

Little Lisa resented my negative feelings about her, and consequently, we were frequently angry at each other. I felt that Little Lisa was a creation of all the attributes that my mother did not love about me. If it was not for Little Lisa, perhaps my mother could have loved me. I wanted to destroy the part of me that my mother hated. I was not willing to try to like anything about Little Lisa, and I was not sure how we were going to continue to exist in the same body while we harbored such an intense dislike for one another.

As different as these four alters were at manifesting themselves, the one thing that united them was their interest in God and their belief in Jesus as the one true Savior for all of humanity. None of them felt the disconnection from God the Father that I did, and none of them saw God in the same mean and punishing way that I felt the Old Testament portrayed. The difference between their view of God and my view of Him confused me because my therapist insisted that their view of Him had to come directly from somewhere within me. "Because they feel connected to God that means you also can feel connected to God," she told me. "You just have to tap into the connection and grab hold of it." She made grabbing onto that connection sound easy, but I had no clue how to do it.

Sensing my frustration over my inability to view God as loving and merciful, Little One had a ready explanation for me. "It seems like you are equating your relationship with God to the relationship that you have with your mother," she told me. "You see God as mean and demanding like your mother. Your mother has caused you to feel unworthy of love for all of your life, and now your sense of self-worth is so low that you don't think you are worthy enough for God to love you."

"How do I fix that?" I cried out. "I want to connect to God the Father and to feel His love for me, but I don't know how. I keep thinking that God expects perfection from me and that I fail Him every day."

"You need to see the difference between your mother and God," Little One said. "It's not fair to God to judge Him based on the way that your mother has treated you. God is not the same as your mother."

"But God seems so mean in the Old Testament," I said. "He expected perfection from the Israelites and then made them sacrifice animals to atone for their imperfections."

Mouse, who had been listening to the conversation, chose that moment to add her unwanted opinion. "God is holy," she said. "When He first made Adam and Eve, He made them perfect. It was not His fault that they decided to sin. God can't stand anything bad."

My frustration was mounting. "So, Adam and Eve ate some fruit after God told them not to," I said. "God kicked them out of their garden for that one mistake. If He did not want them to eat any of that fruit, then why did He put that fruit tree in the garden at all? He had full control over what He put into the garden. He did not have to put that tree in there. It seems like God put that tree in there to tempt them. He set Adam and Eve up to fail, and then He punished them when they did fail. What kind of loving God does something like that?"

"We don't presume to know why God does all of the things that He decides to do," Little One said quietly. "Since you're having so much trouble understanding Him, perhaps the answers is to find a church to attend that will help us learn more about Him."

"Let's go back to Sunday school!" Mouse eagerly agreed.

I had many excuses for why I could not attend church. I was not good enough to go to one. I would not know how to act. I did not have the right kind of clothes to wear. The pastor might expect me to give money to the church that I could not afford to give.

My excuses for not attending church were ignored. If Mouse wanted to do something that she thought would be fun, there was no stopping her. When she threatened to take control of the body and walk around the town until she found a church, I knew that I would have to break down and take her to one. I had a great deal of anxiety about it because not only was I awkward in social situations; I was worried about how Mouse would behave in front of the people there. It was not going to bode well for an adult sized body to try to participate in a children's Bible class.

Not knowing anything about the churches in the area, I picked the first church listing in the telephone book that my I saw. When Sunday morning arrived, and it was almost time to drive to the service, my nerves became more frayed as Mouse gathered up her crayons and scissors in anticipation of doing children's crafts.

"You cannot attend a children's Bible class in an adult-sized body," Little One told Mouse for the millionth time.

"Who says I can't?" Mouse retorted.

"Society says," Little One replied. "It would not be appropriate."

"Would it be against the law?" Mouse asked.

"Just because an action is not against the law does not make it socially acceptable," Little One responded.

"I will tell you what is not acceptable," Mouse said calmly. "People starving is not acceptable. People being abused is not acceptable. And people not being allowed to go to church and enjoy God in their own way no matter what their body size is also unacceptable."

"You can go to church and enjoy God," Little One said hastily. "But you must do it appropriately."

"What will happen if I do it my way?" Mouse persisted. "Will the Pastor have me thrown into jail?"

"You know better than that," Little One said. "The issue is that people would not understand you are acting like a child in an adult body, and that would be embarrassing and cause issues for Lisa."

"I hate to tell you this," Mouse said evenly, "but I do not care what any person in this world thinks. I only care about what God thinks."

"That's it. I am not going to any church," I said frantically.

"I will go by myself," Mouse said.

"But you do not know the way there," Bug said. "We will get lost and die out in the elements."

Mouse ignored that and began to walk toward the door, confidently clutching her crayons and scissors.

I felt caught in a difficult situation. Allowing Mouse to wander all around town would cause more trouble and danger for me than taking her to the church would. I felt angry that I did not have control over the situation. I also felt frightened that I was going to walk into the church and quickly become the freak of the town more than I already thought that I was. "You are not making my first experience with the church a positive one," I said bitterly to Mouse.

"Your attitude is your own choice," Mouse said. "Do not blame me for your negativity."

Little One reached out and grabbed our jacket on the way out the door. "Mouse, if you make this bad for Lisa, I will never forgive you," she warned.

The Spirit of Glory church sat off by itself in the middle of what appeared to be a cornfield. It was a small church, brightly lit, with many cars parked haphazardly around it. As we approached the building, I could hear loud music and other strange noises coming through the windows.

When Bug heard the loud music, she immediately stopped and would not allow us to move any closer to the building. She was easily frightened by noise and chaos after having been through so much of it during my childhood. "I am not going in there," she said meekly. "It is too noisy. I hear too many people."

"I agree," I said. "Let's forget this and go back home."

I tried to turn my body around and make a mad dash back to the car, but Mouse held me there with firm control. She was much stronger about

controlling our body than I was. "There isn't anything to be afraid of in God's house," she said cheerfully as she took a couple of steps toward the door.

"Wait a minute, Mouse." Little One sounded frantic. "Please stop!"

Mouse paused and asked impatiently, "What do you want? You are holding up my fun."

"We need to let Lisa be the one to go into the church," Little One said. "We need to stay quiet and let Lisa have control of the body, just like we let her have control when she is at work."

"If Lisa is in control of the body she will ruin my fun," Mouse complained.

"I am not sure that I want control of the body right now," I admitted. "I am afraid of this whole scenario."

"Please, Mouse," Little One continued. "The people inside the church do not know about us. They will not understand that we also exist in Lisa's body. I want to protect Lisa from people thinking that she is crazy."

"But Lisa is crazy," Mouse said. "They will find out sooner or later."

"I hate to resort to bribery," Little One sighed. "There will be an extra treat for you tomorrow if you let Lisa walk into the church."

Mouse hesitated. She enjoyed getting treats so much that it was often easy for Little One to use them to bribe her into doing things. "Okay, Lisa can walk into the church," she finally agreed.

Once I had control of my body again, fear took me over, and I stood there trembling while I stared at the building. The music and other noise seemed overwhelming. My heart began to thump with anxiety at the thought of facing so many strangers.

"Are you going to stand out here all day?" Little Lisa snapped.

I took a deep breath, and then I opened the door and stepped inside of the church. Several older women in long flowing dresses were standing just inside of the door, and they immediately reached out to hug me the second I stepped inside. "Welcome, sister," one of them said to me.

Bug spoke to me inside of my head. "Is that your sister?" she asked.

I did not like to be touched, so I gave the women a faltering smile and slipped past them. I followed the noise to the sanctuary and stopped in the doorway to survey the scene. People were dancing and skipping around the room, while other people fell writhing onto the floor. I did not have a clue what was going on, but I did not dare step one foot into that sanctuary.

Mouse had entered the church with high confidence and zeal, but now she stood there with trepidation and confusion. "This is not how I remember the church where I went to Sunday school," she said.

"I want to go home," Bug wailed. She spoke aloud, but our conversation went unheard and unnoticed over the noise.

Before I could turn around to leave, one of the women who was dancing close to me rushed over and grabbed my arm. "We are having a Holy Ghost inspired revival here this evening," she told me excitedly.

"Do you have a Sunday school here?" Mouse yelled.

I cringed, but the women seemed to take no notice of the strange way that Mouse talked. "There isn't any Sunday school going on here tonight," she laughed. "We are letting the Holy Ghost work in us tonight."

Mouse was disappointed. She wrenched our arm free from the woman's grasp and said, "I am not going to stay here if there is no Sunday school."

I was relieved when Mouse left the church and went back to the car. Bug looked over her shoulder to see if any of the women were following behind us, but none of them tried to stop us from leaving.

Once inside my car, I locked the doors and sat there trying to comprehend what I had just witnessed. A feeling of unease had settled over me.

"That scared me," Bug said. "I don't ever want to go back to church."

"I don't either," I agreed.

"Are you going to give up on God just because of how the people act in one church?" Mouse asked.

I started the car and headed home. "I could never behave like those people were," I said.

"God did not ask you to behave like that," Mouse pointed out.

"But if that is the type of behavior that God expects from me, I cannot do it," I said.

"Do not judge God based on the way other people act," Mouse said.

"That was nothing more than emotionalism," Little Lisa said. "I do not believe that the Holy Spirit causes people to act that way."

"What is the Holy Spirit?" Bug asked. "Spirits are scary."

"I don't know anything about the Holy Spirit," I admitted.

"The Holy Spirit is part of God," Mouse explained. "There is the Father, the Son, and the Holy Spirit. They are three parts that make up one God." She paused and then giggled. "Sort of like us," she said. "Different parts that make up one person."

That was the first church service that I had ever attended, and I vowed that it would be the last. I knew I would never find God there. If anything, I now felt even more disconnected from Him. I decided if those behaviors were the way that Christians were expected to engage in, then I did not want to be a Christian at all. I could never be like those people. Jesus was my Savior, but I no longer wanted to be considered a Christian. I went away from that church with a worse concept of God than I had before I had gone there.

## Eight

*Therefore do not cast away your confidence, which
has great reward. For you have need of endurance,
so that after you have done the will of God, you
may receive the promise. (Hebrews 10:35-36)*

For two years after attending that church service, I had an on-again, off-again relationship with God. The people at the church had left me with an incorrect view of what it meant to be a Christian. My salvation became about works because I was sure I had to earn it to keep it. Every time I did, said or thought something that I knew to be wrong, I was certain that God would remove my salvation from me, and I would start over again at trying to earn His favor so that I could win my salvation back again. It became an exhaustive cycle, and finally, I decided that keeping my salvation was too much work.  I did not need the constant reminders of what a failure I was.  God was just too demanding, and I could not keep up with His expectations and His standards for living. I put away my bible, took down the pictures of Jesus that I had on my walls, and turned away from God altogether. I had enough to struggle with, and I did not need to add the constant burden of trying to please God to that struggle. I had to part ways with God because trying to please Him was causing my sense of self-worth to stay in the toilet. Jesus had died for me, but I could only keep failing Him.

The more I tried to distance myself from God, the closer Mouse became to Him. She and I were in constant conflict as to how we viewed God. While Mouse saw Him as a loving and merciful God, I saw Him as a demanding tyrant who would quickly send me to hell for any mistake that I made. I understood that the vastly different ways that Mouse and I viewed God were the result of my conflicting thoughts about Him, but it seemed to be a war between Mouse and me as to which view of God was going to prevail.

I struggled a great deal during those years. Not only did I have Multiple Personality Disorder, but I also had the symptoms of Bipolar Disorder, and I had frequent bouts of major depression followed by episodes of hypomania. My psychiatrist changed my medication frequently in attempts to alleviate my debilitating symptoms, but the medications left me with adverse physical side effects.

It was difficult for me to function during these years, and my alters did their best to keep me going. They tried to normalize my reckless and impulsive behaviors, but it was difficult because they were not equipped with all of the functional abilities that I had, such as being able to work or drive the car. With all of my alters trying to function for me, my behavior often appeared erratic and bizarre to the outside world. It was getting difficult to hold onto my job, and I knew that, eventually, I was going to lose my ability to work. The thought of not being able to provide for myself financially became so overwhelming that my depressive episodes increased in severity.

I was in and out of the hospital at various times during those years, mostly short stays to prevent suicide attempts. Multiple Personality Disorder was not widely understood or accepted by the hospital staff at that time, so they usually tried to keep me in a room by myself. During my fourth hospitalization, there were no empty rooms available for me, so I was paired with a roommate. I did not know what they had told my roommate about me, so I encouraged my alters to remain inside as much as possible so as not to distress her with my symptoms.

My roommate was a little wisp of a girl named Kathy. She was three years younger than me, and I found her lying on her bed reading a large print Bible. My heart sank to my knees. *Here we go again,* I thought wearily. *How many times in my life am I going to run into strangers who are Christians?* It seemed the more I tried to ignore God, the more Christians I kept meeting.

Kathy looked at me as I walked into the room. I sat my bag of clothes on my bed and tried to ignore her as I went about putting my clothes into the small drawer next to the bed. "Are you a Christian?" she asked.

"No," I said promptly.

"Darn it," Kathy said. "I told Denny I only wanted Christian roomies."

"I'm sorry they don't adhere to your specific requests," I replied sarcastically. "The last I heard this isn't a hotel."

Kathy closed her Bible and laid it on her bed. "No need to get testy," she said. "I find it easier to get along with other believers. That is all I am saying. Is this your first day here?"

I finished putting away my clothes and sat on my bed. "I have been here for eight days," I told her. "I am hoping to go home in a few days."

"I have been here for two weeks," Kathy said. "No clue when they will open the door for me."

Curiosity got the best of me. "Why are you here?" I asked.

"Let's just say that my temper got the best of me and leave it at that," Kathy sighed. "They are telling me that I'm a sociopath, but I disagree. I can't fight the system though."

I was more than surprised. Up until then, I had never met a Christian with a mental illness. "How can you be a sociopath when you are a Christian?" I asked.

"I do not think I am a sociopath," Kathy said. "Some of these folks around here really do not know their rear ends from a hole in the ground. They think having an education gives them the ability to know everything about everybody. They don't know a damn thing though."

"You cuss!" I said incredulously.

"It is a bad habit," Kathy said. "I know God does not like bad language, but I have not been able to stop it yet. I am working on it though. I am glad that God is so patient with me."

"How do you know that God is patient with your bad habits?" I asked.

"He sent His son to die for my bad habits. That is how I know," Kathy said.

"You must have to get saved one million times a day," I remarked.

Kathy looked confused. "What do you mean?" she asked.

"You know, having to get saved every time you do something wrong," I said.

Kathy laughed at me. "You cannot be serious," she said. "I thought that everybody knew once you are saved, you're always saved. You do not have to ask for salvation more than once. If you believe that Jesus as your Savior, you do not have to ask God for salvation repeatedly."

"What about when you do something wrong?" I persisted.

"All you have to do is ask God to forgive you and try your best not to do it again," Kathy said. "God is merciful and will always forgive us. It is not a matter of having to become saved again. You get saved one time, and after that, it is a matter of forgiveness when you do something wrong."

"How can you be so sure that He forgives you?" I asked. "What if you do something *really* wrong?"

"In the Bible, there was a guy named Paul running around killing Christians," Kathy said. "If God can forgive a murderer of His people He will forgive anything. Well, just about anything. The Bible says the only thing He will not forgive is blasphemy."

"Blasphemy?" I repeated. "What is that?"

"That is when you say slander or libel directed at God," Kathy replied. "It is the outright rejection of Jesus."

At that moment, a nurse stuck her head in the door and announced that it was time for lunch. "Time for chow," Kathy squealed as she jumped off the bed.

I was disappointed because I wanted to talk to Kathy more about the forgiveness of sins. Had I been wrong in thinking salvation depended on how good you behaved each day?

I was still thinking about this later in the evening during my hour of free time. During the day hours, the patients in the psychiatric unit had to attend various groups and counseling sessions, but for an hour after supper, they allowed us to spend the time doing whatever we wanted to do, as long as we did not hibernate in our rooms. I usually spent the hour in the activity room with the other patients who were playing games or reading, but I stayed off in a corner by myself and tried to avoid interacting with anybody. I just wanted to finish my time in the unit and get back home. I had taken a two-week leave of absence from work, and it would be time for me to return in less than a week. The new medications that I was taking seemed to be working. My moods had stabilized, and my depression had lifted enough that I was able to think more clearly. This evening during free time, I sat off by myself and thought about the things that Kathy had told me about God and salvation. She had challenged some of my conceptions about becoming saved and being a Christian. I wondered if perhaps I was placing far more burdens and expectations on myself than God was putting on me.

I was deep in thought about this when I heard Kathy's voice rise among the din. "I do not care if you believe in God or not," she shouted. "Stop calling me a religious freak."

I looked over to see to whom Kathy was talking. She was sitting at a table near me playing cards with three other patients. She was talking to a woman named Joan.

Joan was one of the patients that I did my best to avoid. She was a big and burly middle-aged woman with tattoos all over her arms who looked like she belonged in a motorcycle gang. She was loud, outspoken, and very brash. Most of the other patients tried to befriend her because it was better than being on her bad side. She was always crabby because she was a smoker, and cigarette smoking was not allowed in the unit. I had overheard her trying to convince the nurses to let her go outside long enough to smoke one cigarette, but after having her request denied, she was ready to pick a fight with anybody. She threw her cards on the table and pointed at Kathy. "There is too much evil in this world for there to be a God," she bellowed. "People are getting murdered and raped and kids dying of terminal diseases. What kind of God lets those things happen to innocent people?"

Curious about that myself, I looked at Kathy and waited for her reply.

"God did not make robots," Kathy said. "He made people with free will. Unfortunately, some people choose to hurt other people."

"Can't your God even protect His people?" Joan scoffed. "Christians all over the world are being killed. That is some God you've got there."

"You cannot blame God for what people do," Kathy said. "God wants people to love each other and to be kind to one other. He gives rules for human behavior in the Bible. If people followed His rules, the world would not be in the mess it is in today. It is not His fault that each generation is becoming increasingly godless. He won't force Himself on anybody."

"That was a good answer," I said. I caught myself and quickly put my hand over my mouth.

It was too late. Joan heard me, and she turned to look at me. "Did you say something?" she asked in a rude voice.

I shook my head and looked down at the floor.

"Liar," Joan spat. "I heard you. If you have any balls, you will repeat yourself."

I swallowed and forced myself to look up at her. Conflict of any kind caused me great anxiety. "I thought it was a good answer not to blame God for how people treat each other," I said.

Joan walked around the table and stood in front of me. "Who do you think you are?" she demanded.

I felt my heart thumping in my chest. "I am nobody," I replied.

Joan put her hands on her hips and leaned toward me. "Oh, you are somebody," she said. "You are the biggest self-pitying crybaby in this unit, that's who you are."

"I beg your pardon?" I said.

Joan nodded towards the other patients in the room. "We all know about you," she said. "We have been listening to you all week. You think you have got things so bad. You have a job, a car, and an apartment. Do you know how many of us here have the things that you have? None of us."

"That is not my fault," I stammered. "I have worked hard for the things that I have and…" my voice trailed off.

"Bull crap, you work hard," Joan said. "You have got some luck on your side, and you don't even see it. You do not appreciate what you have."

"That is not luck, she is blessed by God," Kathy said.

"I don't think so," I said. "I am not a Christian anymore."

"You are blind. That's what you are," Joan said. "You walk around here with your face constantly dragging to the floor always feeling sorry for your sad state in life. Well, we all got it bad here honey, not just you. You seem like a self-centered person. You also seem like a smart person. So why don't you get off your pity pot and look at what you do have? Use your brains. See Kate over there? She cannot even tie her shoes without help. You have a chance for life out there, but you cannot look past your misery to see it. Why don't you try looking at somebody else's misery for once? Are you afraid that somebody else's misery might be worse than your own?"

I was stunned into silence. Joan was telling me off in ways that nobody else had ever told me off before. Could she be right? Was I nothing more than a self-centered person who could not see past my world of misery? Was I taking what I did have in life for granted? Did other people see me the way that Joan was seeing me—as a negative and ungrateful person? I began to feel sick to my stomach and sick of myself. I did not want people to see me as Joan saw me. I did not want to live the way that I was living anymore. I had doctors, therapy, and medications; apparently, it was not enough. Those things were only masking my symptoms. I needed something that could help change me on the inside—change my feelings and my attitude about life and myself. I was unable to make those changes by myself. I was powerless to make those changes within myself. As I looked up at Joan standing over me, I knew at that moment how desperately I needed God. I needed Him more than I needed anybody else if I wanted to find meaning in my life and make lasting changes within myself. I needed to turn back to Jesus and go back to trying to find God the Father.

~

Kathy's words about not losing salvation after every sin and Joan's words about how I appeared to other people changed my life that day. I left the hospital determined to find God and to become a better person. The first thing that I did when I returned home was to retrieve my Bible from the back of my closet. The second thing I did was to put my pictures of Jesus back up on my walls. I was not going to give up again. I was going to look at my life differently. I decided that I must have been close to finding God the Father and that was why Satan was trying to get me to destroy myself. I realized then that everybody in the world is in a spiritual battle whether he or she knows it or not. I did not understand much about it, so that first night home from the hospital I dug into the Bible looking for anything that I could find about people fighting a spiritual battle. One of the first Scriptures that I found was 2 Corinthians 10:3: *"For though we walk in the flesh, we do not war according to the flesh."* The second one I came across was Ephesians 6:12: *For we do not wrestle against flesh and blood, but against principalities, against powers, against the rulers of the darkness of this age, against spiritual hosts of wickedness in the heavenly places.*

After going through the Bible to find what I could about spiritual warfare, I began to research whatever I could find about Satan. I read with great interest how Satan was once one of God's most powerful and glorious angels, and how he decided to rebel against God. He wanted to be in a position higher than God was, and a result of that God had thrown him out of heaven down to earth, both he and other fallen angels who chose to worship him rather than worship God. The Bible says in

1 Peter 5:8: *Be sober, be vigilant; because your adversary the devil walks around like a roaring lion, seeking whom he may devour.* Satan's mission on earth is to keep as many people away from God as possible. He still wants to be the ruler of the universe. Did he stand a chance at obtaining the highest title that he so desires? The last book of the Bible revealed to me God's answer to Satan's eventual fate. I found the book of Revelation to be even more confusing to understand than the Old Testament, but I was able to understand the passages related to Satan's final act: *And the devil, who deceived them, was cast into the lake of fire and brimstone where the beast and the false prophet are. And they will be tormented day and night forever and ever.* Revelation 20:10. God is going to be the winner. God was the winner in the beginning, and God will be the winner in the end, no matter how many people Satan manages to win to his side. I knew then that the spiritual war that had started at the beginning of time is still raging today, but that fewer people realize it.

At that moment, I was convinced that Satan wanted me to destroy myself. One more person having died without salvation through Jesus was another victory for him, but it was too late. I was now onto him. I was saved. I had confessed Jesus as my savior a few years earlier. I had turned away from Jesus, but I had not lost my salvation. I was a backsliding Christian, but there was still hope for me. I was still alive. God has spared me, and there was still time for me to try to find Him and to ask Him to help me change my life.

I got down on my knees then and cried out to God. "I have found your Son, now please help me find you," I sobbed. "Help heal the damage I have because of the life that I have led. Help me to remove the hatred and bitterness that fills my heart. I do not want to live like this anymore. I do not want the devil to rule over my life anymore. I believe that you have spared me from death for a reason. Help me to know that reason. Help me to make sense of my life. Help me to trust you, because I have zero trust and faith in anything." I stayed in that position and cried out to God for a long time that night. I felt completely defeated, and I knew that He was my only hope for change.

No angel came to minister to me that night. The heavens did not open up to allow God's audible voice to tell me that everything would be okay. I knew that I still had a tough road ahead of me. I knew that God would not heal the damage to my heart and my psyche immediately. I was still struggling with three legitimate psychiatric disorders. At that moment, while I was pouring out my heart to God, I still felt some emotional disconnection from Him; but I knew that He was there somewhere and that the detachment that I felt was only the result of my psychiatric issues. I was determined to figure out what it was in my mind and in my heart that was causing me to feel so blocked from Him. Even though I could not feel Him there at that moment, my brain knew that He was there, ready to help me find the answers that I needed.

Mouse was ecstatic about my submission to God and my desire to find out who He really is. "I will help you," she told me. "I am a part of you, and I will help you find God."

"I am afraid He won't want me," I sobbed. "I am afraid I cannot be good enough for Him."

"None of us are good enough for Him," Mouse said. "If we were standing on our own, none of us could ever win with God. However, He loves us so much, that is why He sent Jesus to take our punishment. That is what you have to keep focusing on."

"I feel so worthless. I don't feel that God could ever love me," I said.

"Your mother ruined you into thinking that way about yourself," Mouse said. "God does not see you in the way that your mother sees you. He will restore you."

I could not stop crying. "I am a lost cause," I said.

"You have serious self-worth issues and trust issues," Mouse said. "This might be a difficult journey, but I know God will not give up on you."

Little Lisa did not share Mouse's enthusiasm. "Do you think God can heal Lisa?" she asked Mouse. "Because Lisa is a dumb ass."

"God can do anything He wants to do," Mouse replied cheerfully. "If God can create this whole world, He can restore Lisa's heart."

"I do not know about that," Little Lisa said doubtfully, but nobody had more doubts than I did.

# Nine

*You, who have shown me great and severe troubles,*
*shall revive me again, and bring me up again from*
*the depths of the earth. (Psalm 71:20)*

God did not immediately make my life easier after the night that I poured my heart out to Him. In fact, life became even more difficult. The medication that the doctor had given me while I was in the hospital did alleviate my mood swings for a few weeks, but before long, depression was knocking at my door again, and exhaustion was setting in. Every morning I asked God to help me get out of bed and to make it into work. It was becoming more challenging for me to last through the eight-hour shifts. My energy just was not there. It was also becoming more difficult to keep my many symptoms controlled for that long. The mood stabilizing medication that I was taking was causing me troublesome side effects; such as, extreme hand tremors and gait issues. I was losing my balance while walking. My ability to concentrate on anything for more than a few minutes at a time was decreasing, and I noticed a sharp decline in my memory as well. Eventually, it got to the point that on the days that I worked it was all that I was able to accomplish that day.

I prayed each day that God would help me continue working. That job meant everything to me. Work had proven beneficial to me in several ways. Over time, I began to relate to the staff more appropriately, and I conquered my inability to look people in their eyes. My aversion to physical touch had also decreased in the wake of having frequent physical contact while caring for the patients.

The instability of my mental health issues eventually proved to be too costly when it came to work, and I began calling into work sick on the days when no amount of prayer or help from my alters could get me out of bed. Struggling with my symptoms also led me to begin going into my shifts late or leaving early. The staff started to complain about my attendance issues. I was angry with them for their complaints. They had no idea how much force that it took me to put one foot in front of the other on the days that I did manage to get there. They knew nothing about my struggle to focus with a mind constantly filled with distorted thoughts and alters who were continuously having conversations with each other.

I thought that I was invincible with Jesus on my side. I thought that He would make sure that everything would be all right for me, especially because He knew my desire to change myself and to become a better person. He could see how hard I was struggling to keep that job. I was trying so hard to hold up my end of the work, so I was sure He would reward my effort and not let me down. After all, if Jesus loved me, the last thing He would want was for me to lose my job and my apartment and have to return to my dysfunctional family. I was confident that Jesus would see to it that my life would stay the same.

I was wrong. I did end up losing my job. I do not know what shocked me more – losing my job or the fact that Jesus had let me down in such a big way. The despair and anxiety that I felt were off the charts. What was I going to do? With no income, I could not afford to feed myself much less keep my apartment. I felt like Jesus had pulled a fast one on me. My trust in Him seemed only to result in the loss of everything that meant anything to me. Knowing that I now had zero income and no other way to maintain my existence caused me great panic.

That first night after I lost my job, I paced around my apartment the entire night. I decided that since I could not rely on God or Jesus, I would have to think of a solution by myself. "Why, God?" I repeatedly wailed through my tears. "Why did you let this happen to me? I tried my best to trust you, and you let me down. Every morning I prayed for you to help me keep my job and now I have no income at all. I have been trying so hard to change myself, and this is what I get for my effort?" I collapsed into hysterical tears many times that night. I knew that because of my symptoms I would not be successful at another job. I did not want to return to considering suicide again, but the thought of returning to my family brought me back to those thoughts. I hated myself for being so weak.

Mouse kept encouraging me to trust God, but what little trust I had managed to summon disappeared the second I lost my job. Except for Mouse, my other alters were afraid of the possibility of going back to live with my family. I knew that whatever mental health progress I had made since being on my own would be destroyed if I were to go back to my family.

For two days I tried to figure out what I could do about my situation, but try as I might, I could not think of a way to come up with any income. I felt scared and angry with God. I had several conversations with Him which consisted of tears and yelling as I poured out my frustration with Him for failing my trust in Him. Could He not see how difficult it was for me to trust even in things that I could see, much less trust a God that I could not see but also to whom I felt emotionally disconnected?

After two days of pleading with God to give me my job back, I gave up. My tears were spent, and I was exhausted. I had nowhere else to turn, so I threw myself onto my bed and surrendered to Him. As I lay there wallowing in my fear and misery, I recalled how He had answered my prayer about leaving my family. My answer for that had been to win the lottery, but He had responded to it in a completely different way by giving me an apartment that I could afford. My answer to my current situation was to get my job back, but I began to consider that maybe He had a different answer. Perhaps the answer was for me to purchase another lottery ticket. My situation looked so bleak, and my faith was so immature that I was sure

I needed to help God find the answer. It would be a dual project. I would come up with the solution, and all He had to do was perform the miracle. After all, performing miracles was His specialty. I was willing to do all the thinking. If God did not want to give me a winning lottery ticket, then maybe He could produce a wealthy distant relative who could leave me a huge inheritance. I began to feel hopeful as I got out of bed and retrieved my notebook. I made a list of possible answers to my situation. I was making it easy for God to decide which answer that He liked best. When I finished my list, I sat back and waited for my miracle.

I was still waiting for my miracle three hours later when there was a knock at my front door. I did not want to be bothered while I was waiting for my miracle, so I ignored it. When the knocking sound persisted, I became annoyed and pulled open the door. On my porch stood a woman that I recognized as a neighbor who lived across the street. I had seen her outside and said hello in passing, but I had not formally met her. She smiled widely at me when I opened the door. "Hi," she said brightly. "I'm Sue from across the street."

I nodded and impatiently waited for her to tell me what she wanted.

"Is your name Lisa?" she asked.

"I'm sorry," I said quickly. "Yes, that is my name. What can I do for you?"

Sue handed me a flyer. "My husband is the pastor of the church up the street," she said. "The Calvary Church. Are you familiar with it?"

"You are a pastor's wife?" I remarked. "Are you talking about that small church on Upton Street?"

"That's the one," Sue replied. The smile never left her face. "My husband Dave has been the pastor there for nine years. Do you have a church home of your own?"

I remembered my experience at church several years before and hesitated. "No," I said.

"In that case, I would like to invite you to my church," Sue said. Her voice was as bright as the sun as she handed me a flyer. "We are starting a

ladies' bible study next Sunday if you are interested." She gestured toward the paper she had given me. "That's what the flyer is about."

I glanced at the flyer. I did not intend to join a bible study at any church. "Thanks," I mumbled.

"I hope to see you there," Sue said. She turned to leave and then paused. I was about to close the door when she turned to face me again. "By the way, maybe you could help spread the word that we are looking for somebody who would like to make a little money by cleaning our church on Saturday evenings for our Sunday morning services," she said.

I stopped short. "Somebody to clean the church?" I said.

Sue nodded. "We need somebody who can spend two hours or so on Saturday evenings getting the church ready for our services. We had a girl who was doing it, but she recently moved away. We put up a notice at our church, but at this time, none of our members are willing to do it. We are a small church. We've got maybe fifty members."

"Wouldn't you need a cleaning service to do that?" I asked. "Cleaning a whole church sounds like a big job."

"One person can handle it," Sue said. "We just need somebody for general cleaning. It would be vacuuming, dusting, cleaning the two bathrooms, and straightening up the nursery. The girl who was doing it said it would take her two to three hours depending on if we had any activities during the week. We were able to pay her one hundred dollars every week to do it."

"One hundred dollars for three hours of work?" I exclaimed. "That is good money."

"If you happen to know anybody who might be interested, please send them our way," Sue said. "The church office is open on weekdays."

"I will do it," I said eagerly. "I am willing to clean your church for one hundred dollars a week."

Sue looked surprised. "You are?" she asked.

I nodded eagerly. I could have jumped for joy at that moment. Four hundred dollars a month was only about half of what I was making at work, but it was enough to pay the cheap monthly rent for my apartment. Even though it meant I would be involved with a church, I was not going to pass up that offer for anything. I might not be able to afford food or gas for my car or anything else, but it would at least keep a roof over my head for the time being. My miracle had come! Once again, God had answered my prayer in a completely different way than I had expected. Maybe I could trust Him after all!

Sue saw my eagerness and chuckled. "It is going to be a good day if I can tell my husband I found somebody willing to clean the church before our services," she said. "I am glad I did not ignore God's leading to come over and invite you to the ladies' bible study. Do you think you would also be interested in attending that? We would love to have you."

I hesitated. I did not want to attend a Bible study because I was uncomfortable being in groups with strangers, but at that point, I felt a tug of obligation. If Sue was willing to pay me four hundred dollars a month just to clean her church for three hours a week, I did not want to appear ungrateful by refusing to attend her Bible study. I felt some guilt knowing that if I did force myself to attend the Bible study, it would be out of guilt rather than because I wanted to go. "I will check my schedule and see what I can do," I told her.

"Okay," Sue said. "Come over to the church tomorrow during the afternoon sometime and talk to the lady in the office. Her name is Mandy. She will let you know what needs doing as far as the cleaning and where the cleaning supplies can be found. She will also get the information that she will need from you so that we can write you a check every week. Thank you for being willing to help us out."

"Thank you," I said. When I closed the door, I was so choked up with emotion that I could only stand there for a few minutes and take in what had just happened. I was overwhelmed with gratitude to God for taking care of me and amazed at how He had chosen to answer my prayer at just the right moment. I had the answer for paying the rent for my apartment, but I was still going to need His help with paying my utilities and buying food and other expenses. I had no clue how that was going to happen, but at that point, I was beginning to understand that God did not need my input in answering prayers. I was also learning that His answers sometimes did not come right away but always seemed to come just in the nick of time. Anxiety over losing my job had left me exhausted, but I was excited at the prospect of cleaning the church. It was a job I could do on my own where I would not have to force myself to deal with other people. I could work alone and at my own pace. Most importantly, God had saved me from having to go back to living with my family.

~

The Calvary Church was a small church on the corner of a quiet street. When I went there the day after meeting Sue, it was unoccupied other than the church secretary. She welcomed me warmly and showed me around the building. We discussed what duties were expected of me, and after that, she encouraged me to roam around the building on my own and get a "feel" for it.

The church was old and run down. I had an odd sensation of comfort as I wandered around and looked at everything in the various rooms. It was only the second time that I had been in a church, and my reaction to this church was much different from the reaction I had at the first church. The fact that this church was empty probably aided my feeling of comfort, but I also felt drawn there. I had a familiar sense of belonging, the same sense I had so strongly felt the first time that I stepped foot into the nursing home where I worked. I felt like I was in exactly the right place at the right time.

I made my way to the sanctuary and slid into one of the wooden pews. Wearily I rested my forehead on the back of the pew in front of me. I was desperate to understand this whole thing about God. I knew that I was saved and that God had answered some of my prayers, but something about it all was still missing for me. I still did not understand the concept of God the Father. I still saw Him as separate from Jesus, and I still regarded Him in a negative light. I had given up trying to understand the Old Testament by that point. It was still a dry and dull reading to me in comparison to the New Testament. I felt like a half-believing Christian. I could not understand why it was so easy for me to understand and warm up to Jesus but not to God the Father. Perhaps it was because of the beating and the death that Jesus had suffered for my sake. To me, it seemed to be mean that God would have put Jesus through that kind of torture for any reason.

"Finding your way around?"

Sue had stopped by the church to bring some paperwork to the secretary and interrupted my thoughts. She slid into the pew beside me. "Thank you for being reliable and coming by," she said.

"I need the money," I admitted. "I lost my job a few days ago." I caught myself and stopped. I did not open up to people easily, especially ones that I barely knew.

"I am sorry to hear that," Sue said. "I'm glad we can help you out during a difficult time."

I was grateful that she did not pry into my business. "I appreciate the help," I responded quietly.

"I'm certain that it was God who sent me to your door yesterday," Sue said. "Did you check your schedule? Are you able to come to the ladies' Bible study?"

"I do not think I would do well in a Bible study," I said. "I do not know too much about the Bible."

"That is what the study is for," Sue said. "You can learn more about God's word to us. It is not a class where you get graded or anything like that. It is just a small group of women getting together for fellowship and fun. And refreshments," she added.

I hesitated. "I am not always comfortable around strangers," I said.

Sue prodded my side slightly with her elbow. "Once you meet them, they will no longer be strangers," she said lightly. "The Bible study might sound overwhelming to you right now, so what about attending the church service on Sunday morning? You can come check us out and see if you like what we have to offer."

A sense of obligation rose in me again. "I might be able to do that," I said. *If my energy level will allow me to get out of bed,* I thought tiredly.

"Good!" Sue exclaimed cheerfully. "We have two services on Sunday mornings. One is at nine o'clock, and the other is at ten thirty."

"I am not too good in the mornings," I admitted. "I may be able to make the ten thirty-one, but I can't promise."

Sue stood up. "I hope you can," she said. "I have to run now. Did Mandy fill you in on what cleaning needs doing around here? Do you have any questions about it?"

"I think I will be okay," I said.

Sue gave me a short wave as she walked away. "I hope to see you on Sunday morning."

I continued to sit there as I watched Sue walk away. I liked her. She did not make me feel uncomfortable as so many other people did. With a sigh, I stood up and said aloud, "God, I am still in a pickle. You have provided a way for me to keep my apartment, but that is not going to matter if I starve to death in it. I thank you for keeping the roof over my head, but I am going to need more help. I also need more help with finding you and understanding you. I have a feeling that you brought me to this church for more than just to clean it. If you want me to attend a service here on Sunday, I am going to need your help not to feel too depressed or too crazy to get here. You know how awkward I feel in new situations and especially with a bunch of strangers."

God's mercy continued to extend graciously to me that day. On the way home from the church I stopped at the nursing home to collect my final paycheck. While I was there, the Administrator told me that he was going to allow me to keep renting the apartment. It had not occurred to me that I could lose the apartment because they only rented to employees and I was no longer an employee. I had not anticipated THAT blessing.

When I arrived home, I found yet another unexpected blessing. In addition to my regular pay, I was also paid out for the three weeks of vacation pay that I had accrued. That meant that I would have enough money to pay the utilities and to buy food for another month. God was coming through for me, but I was afraid of how close he was leaving me to the edge. I did not realize that it was His way of helping me to learn to trust Him and to depend on Him for my needs as the needs came along. My faith and my trust were on shaky ground. Although God had provided for me for another month, I immediately began to worry about how I would get through the month after that. I was afraid that God would run out of options for helping me—or worse, that He would change His mind and decide that I was not worthy enough to deserve any more of His help after all.

Cleaning the church turned out to be more difficult than I expected it would be. It was not the size of the church that was the problem; it was that my energy level was non-existent. Nevertheless, knowing that it was my only source of income helped me to get there. As tired as I was, I wanted to do a good job to show Sue and God that I appreciated their help.

The secretary at the church was gone, but she had left the main door unlocked for me. It felt strange to be in a church by myself, but I also felt some awe knowing that I was in God's house. One of the rooms had a radio with a tape deck, so I turned on some Christian music to ease the silence. While I vacuumed and dusted, my mind took off with racing thoughts, worries about how I would support myself once the month was over. My trust in God was minimal, and I was certain that He would abandon my cause at any moment.

Thoughtfully absorbed in my worries, I nearly jumped out of my skin when I felt a hand touch my shoulder. A pleasant-looking man stood next to me. He gestured for me to turn off the vacuum cleaner. I did so while at the same time stepping away from him. I did not see anybody with him, and I was not comfortable being alone with a man. Years of sexual abuse as a child had left me very uncomfortable around men. I was awkward and reserved around most of them.

"I did not mean to startle you," the man said as he thrust his hand in my direction. "I'm Pastor Dave. My wife told me that you would be here this evening, so I thought I would run in and introduce myself."

I hesitated and then loosely grasped his hand. "Lisa," I said.

Pastor Dave nodded. "I appreciate that you will help us get ready for the morning services," he said. "Will you be joining us in the morning?"

A pang of guilt caused me to look away from him. "I don't know yet," I replied.

Pastor Dave took a few minutes to tell me a little bit about the background of the church and some of the activities that the members were involved in. When he asked me if I was a Christian, I blurted out, "Jesus is my savior, but I am having trouble finding God the Father."

Pastor Dave looked surprised. "I have never heard anybody tell me that," he remarked. "Do you understand that God and Jesus are the same?"

"So, they tell me, but I cannot get that straight in my mind," I sighed.

Pastor Dave looked concerned and rubbed his chin thoughtfully. "Do you have any thoughts as to why you are having trouble connecting with God?" he asked.

I shook my head and sighed again. "I have not been able to figure it out," I said. "I have tried reading the Old Testament, but God seems so mean and unyielding." I held up my hand. "You do not have to tell me that I have the wrong concept of God. I have already been told that," I added. "But I know what I have read in the Bible."

Pastor Dave glanced at his watch. "I wish that I had time to explore this further with you," he said, "but I am on my way to the hospital to see a sick congregation member. I am interested in talking more about this. Would you like to set up an appointment to meet with me in my office one afternoon this week? We could explore this further, and maybe I could help you figure this out."

I felt myself blushing. "I don't know," I said. I wanted to talk to Pastor Dave more about it, but the idea of being alone in an office with him made me uncomfortable, and I became irritated with myself for hesitating. *Pastors are supposed to be trustworthy,* I scolded myself. *You are not supposed to be afraid of a pastor.* "I feel silly about the whole thing."

"There is nothing to feel silly about," Pastor Dave said. "I would hate for you to miss out on a wonderful relationship with God because you have a concept of Him that does not match His character. I am sure I have some time available on Wednesday afternoon. Would you like to come by around, say, one o'clock?" He seemed persistent, and I felt pressured, but I was curious as to whether He could help me understand and relate to God better. It was difficult for me to agree to spend time alone talking to him because I could not get past the uncomfortable feeling I had whenever I was alone with a man. "You think about it," he said when he saw my hesitation. "My door is open if you decide you want to talk."

"Thanks," I mumbled. "I'll give it some thought."

When I returned home later that evening, I did give it some thought, but I was not sure that I wanted to get too involved with the church or its members. I was afraid that they were going to have expectations of me that I could not possibly meet. When I went to bed that night, I deliberately did not set my alarm clock. I decided that if I overslept in the morning, it would be an as good excuse to miss the church service. My fatigue level was so high that surely God would understand if I overslept.

I did not oversleep. In fact, even without the alarm clock, I was up a full two hours before the first morning service was scheduled to begin. Now I felt guilt mixed with obligation. I was not sure that the congregation at this church would not behave in the same ways that the congregation at Gloria's church had. I felt that I owed God. I knew that He had provided me with income from cleaning the church and the least I could do to show my appreciation was to sit through an hour service. Besides that, I thought I would earn God's favor if I attended the church service. Maybe if I did enough good things, then He would not abandon me.

I entered the church about ten minutes after the service started to avoid having to greet any members who would be curious about a new visitor. To my relief, the small congregation of about fifty people was standing in their places clapping along with the festive worship music that a small band was playing in the front of the church. Nobody was skipping around the church or doing any other behaviors that I would consider bizarre. I relaxed a little bit and slid into the last pew, which was devoid of people. I intended to stay for a short while and then slip out undetected so that I could at least honestly say that I had been there.

I enjoyed the music and the friendly feel of the small congregation so much that I forgot about leaving early and ended up staying for the entire service. Pastor Dave gave a riveting sermon about trusting God through trials that fit my situation so well that it seemed his sermon was directed personally to me. I was shocked when the service ended, and I found myself sitting there basking in a feeling of enjoyment. Even more than enjoying it, I felt drawn to it. In the end, I found myself wishing that it had gone on longer. I was the first one out the door because my discomfort when it came to meeting new people outweighed my enjoyment of being there. Still, I left there feeling excited that the service had been so good for me. I knew without a doubt that if I could manage to force myself out of bed again the following Sunday that I was going to be at that church again.

~

"Excuse me, Pastor Dave?"

Pastor Dave looked up from the papers that he was shuffling on his desk and his eyes lit up with recognition. "Hello there!" he said in a booming voice.

I felt my body trembling with anxiety as I lingered in the doorway. "You said...you said I could stop by this afternoon...to talk," I stammered. My voice sounded weak and far away.

"Certainly," Pastor Dave said, "You've caught me at an opportune time. Come on in and have a seat. You can close the door behind you."

"I would rather leave it open," I said. I would feel safer having an open escape route.

"Whatever you feel more comfortable with," Pastor Dave said as he nodded toward the two chairs sitting in front of his desk.

I hesitated and began to twist the button on my blouse nervously. *One foot in front of the other,* I told myself. I was not sure if I was doing the right thing by talking to him.

Pastor Dave patiently waited until I had crossed the room and sat down. "I saw you at the service yesterday morning," he remarked. "What did you think of it?"

I continued to fiddle with my button and looked at the floor. "I enjoyed it," I replied. "I especially liked your sermon."

"I hope that means you will come again," Pastor Dave said. "What can I do for you today?"

I took a deep breath and made myself look at him. "It's about my issue of not feeling connected to God the Father," I started slowly.

"Ah yes," Pastor Dave said. "I find it interesting that you perceive God and Jesus in such different ways. Perhaps I can help you figure out why you view God in such a negative light. Did you grow up in a Christian family?"

"Not at all," I said. "God did not exist in my family except as a cuss word. In fact, your service was only the second time that I have ever been to church."

"Would you feel comfortable sharing with me a little bit about your family background?" Pastor Dave asked. When I hesitated, he added, "It might be pertinent in the way you have been shaped to perceive God. Is there a history of any abuse in your family background?"

I was reluctant to share anything about my family or myself with him. I knew that he did not have hours to listen to the stories of abuse and trauma that were locked into my mind, and I was not there to obtain his pity. I was there only to see if he could help me to find God. "There was abuse," I admitted quietly.

Pastor Dave seemed unphased, as though he was used to hearing stories about abuse—and I knew that he probably was. "Physical, emotional or sexual?" he prodded gently.

"All three of them," I said. "Mostly at the hands of my mother and my Grandfather."

"I see." Pastor Dave rubbed his chin and gave me a thoughtful look. "Are you still involved with your family currently?" he asked.

"My Grandfather died many years ago," I replied. "I do still have some contact with my family because I love my two younger brothers. My relationship with my parents is not good. I have a lot of hatred in my heart for my mother."

For the next half hour, Pastor Dave talked to me specifically about my mother. He told me how destructive such hatred could be to my life, that God could free me from such hatred, and that He could even help me forgive my mother for all the emotional damage that she had caused me. I had serious doubts that even God's power could not touch the venom in my heart toward her. At that point, forgiving her was not an option for me. She did not deserve my forgiveness, and I did not want to entertain the idea of it even for one minute.

Eventually, my talk with Pastor Dave ended. I had shared more with him than I intended to. Although it was a relief to me to be able to share some of my emotional burdens when our conversation ended, I still did not feel any more connected to God than I did before we talked. Before I left Pastor Dave asked me if he could pray for me and I obediently allowed him to do so. He prayed for me to be able to understand and connect with God, and for God to heal my damaged heart.

As I stood up to leave Pastor Dave said, "Two things did occur to me while we were talking, Lisa. One thing is that you have a negative concept of males because of the sexual abuse you went through. You said you feel awkward and uncomfortable around males. God is perceived as masculine, so perhaps that has something to do with your inability to connect to Him."

I paused for a moment to consider that. "There could be some truth to that," I agreed. "But Jesus is a male, and I love Him."

"You view Jesus in a more submissive and sympathetic way," Pastor Dave pointed out. "You don't see him as a threat in any way. The other thing that I observed is how parallel the way that you view God is to the way that you view your mother. You see both as mean and demanding, unable to be pleased and of quick to punish. That could be a fair assessment of your mother, but it is not a fair assessment of God."

I was startled by his words. My alters said similar things to me. Was it true that I was unfairly comparing God to my mother? If so, how could I possibly change that way of thinking about Him? Pastor Dave had given me food for thought to think about. "Thank you for your time today," I told him.

"I am not a licensed professional therapist," Pastor Dave warned. "You may need to seek out a professional Christian therapist."

"I already do see a therapist," I said.

"Is your therapist a Christian?" Pastor Dave asked. "You would probably do best with some Christian-based therapy to help you better understand God's role in your life."

"I am not exactly getting Christian-based therapy," I replied, "but I have been seeing this particular therapist for several years, and I do know that she believes in God."

"Well, my door is always open," Pastor Dave said. "You may want to make an appointment through Mandy first because I usually stay fairly busy."

"Thanks," I said, "but I don't want to treat you like another therapist."

"Different roles," Pastor Dave smiled. "Will you be returning to service this Sunday?"

"I think so," I said, and then I headed home to think about all that had transpired for me during the past two weeks.

# *Ten*

*But as it is written: "Eye has not seen, nor ear heard, nor have entered into the heart of man the things which God has prepared for those who love Him." (1 Corinthians 2:9)*

A week after talking to Pastor Dave I went to see my therapist. It was the first time that I had seen her since losing my job, and I was still feeling anxious and in a quandary about what I should do. I was not keen on looking for another job because I did not think that I would fare any better at a different job than I had at the nursing home. The symptoms of my psychiatric disorders combined with the harsh side effects of my medications were still making even simple daily tasks difficult for me. I was willing to try another occupation. I had to because I was sure that God's provisions for me would soon run out. "I would rather try to commit suicide again then end up back with my family," I told my therapist.

"I agree that the last thing we want is for you to go back to your family," my therapist said. "Are you still having suicidal thoughts?"

"I have suicidal thoughts almost every day," I admitted. "You know that I am not too fond of life. I don't think I will ever understand it."

"Suicidal thoughts have become a coping skill for you," my therapist said. "Some people use alcohol or drugs to cope with the stress in their lives, but you use suicidal thoughts to cope with yours. We need to find healthier coping skills for you."

"I've been going to a church," I said. "I like it."

"That's great," my therapist said. "Many people find meaning in their life through their faith."

"I haven't found either meaning or faith yet," I sighed.

"On a scale of one to ten, with ten being the highest, how much of a danger are you to yourself?"

I sighed again. My therapist asked me that same question nearly every time that I saw her because of my history of suicide attempts and self-mutilation. Often, I tried to hide the real answer to that question to avoid another stint in the hospital. Because of my past, I would be considered a suicide risk by the psychiatric profession for the rest of my life. "Maybe four," I told her.

My therapist regarded me carefully, searching my face to determine whether I was truthful. One of the reasons that I liked her so well was because it was difficult for me to pull the wool over her eyes. I also liked her because she was devoted to helping me improve the quality of my life, and she remained determined and devoted to me no matter how hopeless I became. Now I watched as she relaxed, trusting that I was truthful about my danger level. "Four," I repeated, "but that number will become considerably higher if I don't find another job soon. I can't survive without income."

"I have an idea about that," my therapist said thoughtfully. "Lisa, I don't believe that you should be trying to hold a job at this point in your life. You have serious psychiatric disorders, and your symptoms have been unstable for quite some time. I believe you should be putting your effort into therapy right now."

"Therapy doesn't pay the bills," I said sarcastically.

"I think you would be eligible for disability," my therapist stated. "I think your psychiatrist and I would have a good case for getting you on disability benefits. That way you could use your effort to concentrate on your therapy."

"Disability?" I said. "How would I go about that?"

As my therapist explained more about disability income, I had a knee jerk reaction at first. While not having to go to work each day while struggling with symptoms and medication side effects sounded like blessed relief, it also cemented the fact to me that I had psychiatric disorders so disabling that I could not function like a normal person. "Who decides what is normal?" my therapist asked me after I had questioned her about it. "What is normal looks different for everybody. You happen to have some extensive limitations that affect your ability to work at this point in your life."

I like to research things especially before I make big decisions, so I went home and studied what disability was all about. While I had worked long enough to qualify for benefits, I was discouraged to read that up to 85% of first-time applicants are denied benefits, and then I would have a lengthy appeal process to handle. The appeal process could include mountains of paperwork and hiring a lawyer to represent me in front of an appellate judge. I did not have the stamina nor the energy to put up such a fight to win the benefits. Nevertheless, my therapist encouraged me to fill out the initial paperwork, and she and my psychiatrist would take care of sending any medical records that were requested. After I applied for disability, I went back to worrying about how I was going to survive. I knew that it could take up to six months before I received a decision about disability, and I was convinced that I would be denied like most first-time applicants were.

While I waited for the disability decision, I continued to clean the church every Saturday evening and then to attend service on Sunday mornings. What kept me going to the church was my growing love for Jesus. I felt overwhelmed every time I thought about Him going to the cross for my sake. Whenever I took communion, I would end up with tears streaming down my face. The more that I learned about Jesus, the more that I loved Him, and the more convinced I was that I had done the right thing by accepting Him as my savior. I wanted to live my life in a way that would make Jesus proud of me, but my sagging sense of self-worth and my inability to find meaning in my life left me feeling hopeless and depressed. Every time Pastor Dave gave a sermon about becoming a new person in Christ, I felt discouraged. I had a strong desire for change, but I did not know how to make it happen.

"God doesn't usually change people or circumstances overnight," Pastor Dave told me when I mentioned the lack of change in my situation. "It's usually a gradual process."

"Why?" I wailed. "God made the universe in six days, so why does He drag His feet when it comes to changing my life?"

"I don't think anybody can ever really understand why God chooses to work in our lives the way that He does," Pastor Dave replied. "Our job is to have faith enough to trust Him during the journey no matter how difficult it is or how long it takes."

"Spoken by a pastor," I sighed.

"Even pastors have to learn to trust God enough to wait on Him," Pastor Dave chuckled. "Life can become stressful and frustrating for pastors too."

I felt like I was running in a circle when it came to God. I knew that salvation was a gift from God straight from His grace and mercy, but I still kept trying to earn His approval. Every time that I failed Him, I would ask for His forgiveness, but I never truly felt forgiven. I continued to carry the heavy burdens of guilt and failure on my shoulders. By then I realized that I was viewing God in the same negative ways that I viewed my mother, but no matter how I tried, I could not change my way of thinking about God. It was trying to understand the Old Testament that had turned me off from Him.

"That just doesn't make sense," Pastor Dave told me. "How can you think of God as cold and harsh when He is the one who sent Jesus to earth to die for you so that you could become reconciled to Him?"

I was so flustered by it all. "I just can't get my mind to think right about it," I said.

"I can only advise you to continue seeking Him," Pastor Dave said. "Keep praying for Him to open up your mind so that you can understand

Him. Perhaps you would feel more connected to Him if you became more involved in church activities. I understand that you are not comfortable in social situations, but perhaps you should consider joining a Bible study. They can be very beneficial to new and growing Christians. There is a list in the foyer of the studies that are currently going on here at the church. Why don't you check it out and see if one of them might interest you?"

I went out to the foyer and looked at the list of studies. There were no groups that were studying anything from the Old Testament, but there was a study from the book of Revelation that did interest me. I was fascinated with that last book in the Bible even though I did not understand much of it. The study was held at the church on Wednesday evenings. After giving it some thought, I decided that I would try to override my social anxiety enough to join the group. The small congregation was no longer new to me. Even though I rarely conversed with any of them outside of saying "hello" or "God bless you," by then I recognized most of them and knew some of their names.

~

When Wednesday came, I had yet another fight on my hands when it came to getting to the church for the Bible study. It seemed that whenever I tried to do anything at the church, my symptoms or my medication side effects would become worse. I began to think of this as a sly tactic by the devil to keep me out of the church, so I tried to push through it. My medications caused me to feel sick most of the time. I had chronic gastric issues, blurred vision, and weakness in my muscles, as well as trembling and balance issues. On this particular morning, I felt tired and nauseated, but I forced myself to go to the church. "Not today, Satan," I said as I headed out my door. "Not today."

There were more people at the Bible study than I had anticipated. Eighteen people crammed into the small room and squeezed together at three oval shaped tables. I was greeted, but nobody made a fuss about me being there, and I was grateful. I blended in with the crowd. Nobody seemed to notice my trembling hands as I opened my Bible to the book of

Revelation. I was still using the little Bible that Gloria had given me years before.

One of the group members started the study by praying for wisdom and understanding and then a discussion began with Revelation chapter 21. I quickly realized that I had missed most of the study and the group was already near the end. I thought about leaving since I was so far behind. I was sure that I would not understand what they were going to talk about since I had missed so much from the beginning of the book. In the end, I decided to stay because I did not want to disrupt the group with an untimely departure. Therefore, I sat there and followed along as one of the members began to read the chapter.

*And I saw a new heaven and a new earth, for the first heaven and earth had passed away. Also, there was no more sea.*

*Then I, John, saw the holy city, the New Jerusalem, coming out of heaven from God, prepared as a bride adorned for her husband.*

*And I heard a voice from heaven saying, "Behold, the tabernacle of God is with men, and He will dwell with them, and they shall be His people, and God Himself will be with them and be their God.*

*And God will wipe away every tear from their eyes; there shall be no more death, nor sorrow, nor crying; and there shall be no more pain, for the former things have passed away."* Revelation 21:1-4

I stopped listening at that point, and with a trembling finger, I went back and read those scriptures over again. I felt utterly overwhelmed and marveled greatly at what I was reading. In the future, God is going to make a new heaven and a new earth for His people. It will be a place where no death, pain or sorrow exist. It took every fiber of my being to keep myself from jumping out of my chair at the joy that I felt at that moment. The group member was still reading, but I kept going back to read those same verses repeatedly. How had I missed such an incredible promise from God the Father for so many years? It is a promise so full of hope that I could hardly contain my excitement. Could this promise have come from the same cold, harsh God who laid down so many strict rules and laws in the

Old Testament? Here He promises us a new heaven and a new earth in the future. A perfect sin free place where His people—those who have accepted Jesus as their savior—will live with Him. There will be no crime on that new earth. No poverty. No disease. No death! My trembling became more pronounced, but it was not from the medication side effects. This time my tremor was coming from the hope and excitement that suddenly filled my heart.

I was eager to get home so that I could continue to read at my own pace. Once I did return home, I immediately sat down and read the entire chapter of Revelation 21 very carefully. My feeling of excitement and marvel continued all the way until the end verses:

*And I saw no temple in it, for the Lord God Almighty and the Lamb are its temple.*

*And the city had no need of the sun or of the moon to shine in it, for the glory of God illuminated it, and Lamb is its light.*

*And the nations of those who are saved shall walk in its light, and the kings of the earth bring their glory and honor into it.*

*Its gates shall not be shut at all by day (there shall be no night there) and they shall bring the glory and the honor of the nations into it.*

*But there shall by no means enter into it anything that defiles, or causes an abomination or a lie, but only those who are written in the Lamb's Book of Life.* Revelation 21:22-27.

I rejoiced then because I knew that my name is written in that Book of Life. My name was written on it the moment that I had accepted Jesus as my savior. I was going to be able to share in the new heaven and the new earth in the future!

God's promises in Revelation helped me to view death in an entirely different way. For most of my life, I had thought of death as annihilation— when you die you cease to exist. I had grieved over the loss of deceased relatives and had seen many other people crumble with despair and devastation over the loss of their loved ones. At one time death meant permanent separation to me, but Revelation changed that. Now I believe that not only do people exist forever once they are born, but I also believe that even dead people still can have hope – the hope of God's promises in Revelation, that they will one day be restored with an incorruptible body to live on God's incorruptible new earth. I know that the Bible states there are different levels of heaven, and I am convinced that dead people who were saved by Jesus are now residing in one of those levels of heaven, waiting for God to make good on His future promises.

That night I thanked God that I was spared from suicide. If I had died without salvation, I would not be allowed to partake of God's planned future. I still struggled with frequent suicidal impulses, so I asked God to help me stand strong against those desires. I now wanted to rely on God to help me through all of my hardships in life, and I wanted Him – not me – to decide when my life on this earth would end. However, I knew that wrestling with suicidal ideations would probably remain difficult for me because of my propensity for major depressive episodes. The best that I could do at that moment was to ask Him for His help with it, and I was sincerely honest about my request. I knew that He was the only one who could ultimately save me from destroying myself.

Revelation 21 and 22 transformed my thinking about life and death in several ways, and it gave me a basis for hope that I never had before. However, I knew I still had work to do when it came to an understanding and connecting with God the Father. I now understood the beginning, that God had created the universe. I understood the ending: that God is going to restore His people to new bodies and create a new earth for them to reside on. I still did not understand the middle. How did the harsh God of the Old Testament become the good God at the end of the New Testament? Would I ever overcome my feeling of disconnection with Him? All I could do was to keep seeking Him. I felt that over the years He had been pursuing me and that He was revealing Himself to me little by little.

# Eleven

*Do not be afraid of sudden terror, nor of trouble
from the wicked when it comes. For the Lord will
be your confidence and will keep your foot from
being caught. (Proverbs 3:25-26)*

Finding the joy and hope of God's future promises soon took a back seat, as my income became a serious concern again. I managed to stretch my last paycheck for almost two months, but after that, my bank account was empty, and I only had the sparse income from the church left to survive on. I tried to leave my income situation in God's hands, but there had been no miracle to aid me. As my money kept dwindling, I began to seek out food pantries and programs that would help me pay my utility bills. If that was going to be God's answer to me, then I prayed that He would help me find the right programs to help me. All throughout the third month, I made it through with help from God in various ways. I sometimes felt discouraged, but I refused to give up. Sheer determination not to have to return to my family kept me going, but it was not easy. I paid my rent with the church income and then relied on other people and programs for everything else. I was grateful for the help that I received, but I was always anxious about where my next meal would come from. I found it difficult to trust God, but I found solace in one of the scriptures: *Be anxious for nothing, but in everything by prayer and supplication, with thanksgiving, let your requests be known to God; and the peace of God, which surpasses all understanding, will guide your hearts and your minds through Christ Jesus.* Philippians 4:6-7.

The day finally came when I received a letter from the disability department in the mail. I was afraid to open it. I knew to expect the usual first-time denial letter, and I did not think that I had the emotional strength to fight the government. I was in for a shock when I did read it. I was approved for benefits! The monthly benefit that I would receive would be slim, but it would be enough to sustain my needs. The first thing that I did after reading it was to thank God. The second thing I that I did was to collapse from the exhaustion of riding with such extreme anxiety for so long. Although I was greatly relieved that I was approved, I also felt sad about it. I knew that my situation was debilitating to have been approved on the first try, but I also knew that it was not because I got lucky. I had many years of documented mental health history behind me that had bolstered my case.

Although I was exhausted, I felt good that day. God had come through for me once again, and I would not have to worry about my bills for a while. I could go on with my therapy and with seeking God and maybe, *just maybe*, things would go right in my life.

Then there was a knock at my door.

I opened the door, and there they stood: my mother, father, and my youngest brother Donnie. Behind them, I could see their car filled with boxes and piles of clothes. My mother looked at me and said grimly, "We were kicked out of our apartment, and we need a place to stay."

My world went dark, and I think I fainted.

When I opened my eyes, I found my brother looking down at me with a concerned look on his face. "What is the matter with you?" he asked.

He should not have had to ask. He should have immediately known what was wrong with me. I loved him dearly, but he was a 21-year-old drug addict with no aspirations in life, and I did not want him staying with me. I did not want any of them staying with me. It was my worst nightmare come alive–to have my family show up on my doorstep homeless and destitute.

My mother stepped around me and looked around my apartment. "Your father and I will stay in your second bedroom," she said. "Donnie can take the couch."

"Wait a minute," I hastily said as I scrambled to my feet. I felt like all of the blood had drained out of my body. "Why did you get kicked out of another apartment?"

"Why do you think?" my mother retorted. "Your useless father did not pay the rent again."

My father came inside followed closely by Donnie. "I don't see your lazy self out looking for a job," he told my mother.

"Wait. Wait." I held up my hands as if to ward them off. "Do any of you currently have any income?"

"I have a back injury," my dad replied. "I'll be getting workman's compensation checks soon."

"When?" I asked frantically.

"Couple of weeks," my dad shrugged. "We thought we would stay here until the checks start coming."

"And then what?" My voice sounded as desperate as I felt.

"Then we will find another apartment," my dad said.

"Don't count on that," my mother said sarcastically. "I think we have already been kicked out of every apartment in town, thanks to you. Donnie, go and get the clothes out of the car."

I blocked the door so that Donnie could not get past me. "I don't think…this is not a good idea," I stammered. "It's not a good idea for any of you to stay here."

My mother put her hands on her hips and glared at me. "Do you expect us to live in our car?" she asked.

I wanted to scream at her: *yes! It is your fault that you keep getting kicked out of your apartments! Go live in your car!* As usual, I was too intimidated to stand up to her. "I think there is probably something in my lease that prohibits me from having other people living with me," I said lamely.

"Then don't say we are living here," my mother retorted. "Just consider us guests for a few weeks."

My stomach sank to my knees. My apartment was supposed to be my safe place away from these people, and they were invading it without even asking for my permission. I knew that they would anchor themselves and never want to leave. With none of them having any income, I also knew that they would soon try to leech off my newly acquired disability benefits. They had just ruined any relief and happiness that I had found. This was not going to end well. I began to chew my fingernails, which was a habit that I had when I was feeling stressed. "Are you sure it will only be for a few weeks?" I asked anxiously.

My mother waved her hand at me. "Sure," she said.

Donnie pushed me aside. "I will empty the car then drive back to get the rest of the boxes," he said.

I watched in horror as Donnie and my father made several trips emptying out their car. They piled boxes in my living room and kitchen. The last thing that my father brought in was a case of beer. "I prefer no drinking or drugs here," I told him.

My mother's eyes challenged mine. "Really?" she said.

I went into my bedroom and closed the door. I could hear my family making themselves at home, as I fell to my knees and clasped my hands in front of me. "God, please help me again," I prayed feverishly. "Please get them out of my apartment, even if it means you have to strike all three of them dead right now. I need you so much right now, God. You know I am too weak to stand up to them. Having them here is going to kill me. I will gladly give up my disability benefits if you will get them out of here."

God did not strike my family dead, nor did He remove them from my apartment. God was silent, and I wondered if He was even there. My disconnection from Him felt greater at that moment than it ever had felt before. God's silence left me with suicidal thoughts flooding my mind. I felt like I was in bondage to my family again. I felt helpless, and the worst of it was knowing that I was allowing them to invade my sanctuary. I hated myself for my weakness. Just an hour before I was feeling some semblance of relief and hope, but the devil had other plans for me. Satan was using one of the most potent weapons in his arsenal to drag me back down. When it came to my family, I was like Superman around kryptonite. "God, I thought you had my back," I cried. "I thought that you do not give your people more than they can bear. If this is some test, I have already failed. Since you won't strike my family dead, then please strike me dead instead!"

God did not strike me dead either. Instead, I was greeted with more silence. In desperation, I reached for my Bible. Pastor Dave had told me to read scriptures, particularly the book of Psalms, when I needed God during a time that I was feeling disconnected from Him. I was trembling as I looked through the Psalms seeking comfort and strength. *My soul waits silently for God alone, for my expectation is from Him. He only is my rock and my salvation. He is my defense; I shall not be moved.* Psalm 62:5-6.

If I was upset about my family's arrival, my alters were furious. Little Lisa was the angriest. She would have confronted my family and demanded that they leave if Little One had not talked her out of it.

"They have no right to be here," Little Lisa fumed. She dropped the Bible on the bed and began to pace around the room. "It takes some nerve for them to come to Lisa for rescue."

"I know, but if you confront them you will make the situation worse for Lisa," Little One said. "Try to calm down so that we can figure this out rationally."

"Nothing is rational when it comes to Lisa's mother," Little Lisa retorted. "If you do not want me to throw them out, then Lisa has to get enough guts to do it herself. Those people cannot stay here."

The thought of standing up to my mother was so overwhelming that I thought I would pass out from the anxiety. Little Lisa still had control of

the body, and she sat back down on the bed when she felt my legs weaken. She was disgusted by my weakness.

"Let Little Lisa deal with my family," I begged Little One. "I cannot do it."

"What can your mother do to you now?" Little One asked. "You are an adult. You are allowing her to have power over you that she no longer."

"No matter what my age, she still frightens me," I said. "Please do not make me feel any more shame than I already feel. I know what my mother is capable of."

"We all know what she is capable of," Little Lisa said sarcastically. "That is why I do not want her to stay here. You will allow her to abuse you."

My high level of distress elicited a similar level of empathy from Little One. Sensing that I was close to my breaking point, she was desperate to figure out a way to manage the situation before I lost what was left of my sanity. She glanced at the Bible lying on my bed and murmured, "Your family needs Jesus."

"Never mind my family. I am the one who needs Jesus right now," I moaned.

Little One's thought had taken root. "I am serious," she said. "If you do not feel strong enough to make your parents leave, then perhaps you can share your faith with them."

Little One's suggestion surprised me so much that for a few minutes I was unable to speak. The thought of sharing Jesus with my family was ludicrous.

"Think about it," Little One encouraged. "You can turn this situation around for good. God wants everybody to hear His message of salvation. Consider what God's love means to you and how it could impact your family as well."

I tried to ignore my anxiety as I considered Little One's idea carefully. Sharing salvation with my family seemed safer than trying to make them leave my apartment. I would do anything to avoid upsetting my mother.

The more that I thought about it, I decided that I did not want my family them to die unsaved. I did not want them to spend eternity separated from God, not even my mother, as much as I hated her. In my heart, I knew that Jesus loved my mother too, even though I wasn't sure why. In my eyes, my mother held no redeeming qualities, but perhaps God could see something in her that I might never be able to see. I asked God for the strength to share Jesus with them. It was going to be a tall order to allow them to stay with me even just for a few weeks. There was no way that I could pull it off without God's help. I was terrified. Dealing with my family always made my psychiatric symptoms worse. Nothing brought suicidal and homicidal thoughts to my mind faster than dealing with my mother did.

I realized then that using this horrible situation as an opportunity to share Jesus with my family would effectively turn the tables on Satan. I knew that he was using my family to try to thwart my efforts to connect with God the Father. Satan knows what type of blows will hit people the hardest. Bringing my homeless family to my door was the best strategy for him to use against me at that time. I was glad that I had developed enough spiritual wisdom to see his tactics. He had dealt me a knockout punch, but I was determined to stand up before the referee could count to three. It was up to me whether I was going to stay down for the count or stand up for the win. Even though I was feeling depressed and anxious, I was going to stand up for the win because I knew that I had the best coach that a fighter could ever have—Jesus.

Satan nearly defeated me that day, but in the end, God used the situation to show me that I was indeed growing spiritually. I knew that my only defense in this battle was going to be to stay close to Jesus and to keep seeking a relationship with God the Father.

~

The first two days with my family staying in my apartment passed uneventfully. Things were relatively quiet, and I stayed in my bedroom reading the book of Psalms as much as I could. The third day offered the first opportunity for me to share Jesus with them. It was Saturday, and I invited my father and Donnie to help me clean the church.

They both looked surprised. "You clean a church?" my dad asked.

I explained to him that I was paid to clean a church for Sunday services, and if they wanted to help me clean it that evening, I would allow them to have the money for doing it. Because they were without income, I assumed that they would both jump at the offer. However, Donnie made it clear that he wanted no part of being at any church. "I'm an atheist," he informed me.

"Why?" I asked.

"Don't start preaching at me," Donnie retorted. "I do not believe in God."

"Why?" I persisted.

"Your brother does not have to explain his beliefs to you," my mother spoke up. "Leave him alone about it."

I turned to her. "Do *you* believe in God?" I asked her.

I braced myself and waited for her to tell me off. She rarely spoke to me decently. The tension was usually thick between us. To my surprise, she managed to answer me calmly. "I don't know if there is a God or not," she said. "I do not waste time thinking about it."

"You should," I told her. "Don't you care what will happen to you after you die?"

"I do not give a damn what happens to me after I die," my mother said flatly. "Don't preach at me either. How did you end up this way? I always knew you would not end up like the rest of the family."

"Why? Because I never have drunk alcohol or taken drugs?" I asked.

"Because you're turning into one of those pesky holier than thou people," my mother replied sharply.

"I am not," I said. "I am just trying to share Jesus with you all."

"Share Him with somebody else," Donnie said.

I pressed on. "Do any of you know what Jesus did for you?" I asked.

"Can't you get it through your thick head that we do not care?" my mom said.

My father had remained silent during the exchange, so I turned to him. "What about you, Dad?" I asked. "Do you believe in God?"

"I have watched that movie The Ten Commandments a few times," my father replied. "The one with Charlton Heston in it."

"Really?" I said hopefully.

"I thought it was a good movie," my father offered.

"Who are you kidding?" my mother said. "You do not believe in God any more than the man on the moon does."

I stayed focused on my father. Maybe there was a chance for him. "Do you want to help me clean the church?" I asked. "You can have all of the money if you help me."

My father hesitated. "I have a back injury," he reminded me.

"It doesn't seem that bad," I said. "You did manage to carry those heavy boxes up the stairs. It is not heavy cleaning. It's vacuuming and dusting, things like that."

My father relented. "I will help you if you give me the money for doing it," he said.

With my father helping me to clean the church that evening, I was able to pursue talking more about Jesus with him. Since my father and I did not have much of a relationship and rarely spoke more than a few sentences to each other, our conversation seemed awkward, but I was able to share the message of salvation with him. He seemed interested in what I was saying, but I did not know if he would ever really do anything with the information that I was giving him. Still, I was relieved that God had allowed me to share it with him. At least it provided him with the knowledge to make his own choice about his salvation. "How did you get into this religion stuff anyway?" he asked me while we were cleaning the church nursery.

I remembered Gloria and said, "A friend told me about Jesus, and I believed it right away."

"Your Grandparents were Catholic," my father mentioned casually. "Your mom's parents. They raised your Aunt and Uncle in the Catholic religion, but they did not raise your mother in it."

I was shocked. It was the first time that I had ever heard of any religion being anywhere in my family. "I never heard any of them speak about God," I pointed out. "They never went to church."

"They all fell away from it before you were born," my father explained.

"Why didn't they raise mom that way?" I asked.

"I don't know," my father replied, "We never talked about it." He stopped what he was doing and looked at me. "Your mother did not have an easy childhood," he said. "There was a lot of drinking and violence."

"Then why did you two give me the same kind of childhood?" I cried out. "My entire childhood was taken from me by your drinking and violence. And mom blames her own horrible life on me being born!"

"I'm sorry," my dad said.

"You are sorry?" I raged. "What good does your apology do for me now? Sorry does not cut it, Dad. I have all kinds of mental and emotional problems. I can barely function most days. Look at this." I held out my trembling hands. "I am sick all the time from the medications that I have to take," I told him angrily. "I will probably have to take these medications for the rest of my life. I never feel good. I cannot even work a job like a normal person! This is what you and mom have turned me into, and I hate you both for it!"

My father was silent for a moment, and then he picked up a cloth and slowly began to wipe the toy table. "Your mom was right when she said you are different from the rest of the family," he said quietly.

"How am I different?" I asked. "I may not drink alcohol or take drugs like the rest of you do, but I am just as screwed up as you all are. I will probably never be able to have a normal life. I will never get married or have children."

"Lisa, from the very day that you were born, we knew that you would be different from us," my father said. "You have always had some light within you. That is why you have clashed with your mother from day one. This family is full of darkness, and your light has never belonged with that darkness. You say you are not different, but you have also told me in the past that you feel like a complete outcast in this family. That is because you *are* an outcast. You also said that you are the black sheep in the family, but the opposite of that is true. You are a white sheep among us. A sheep among wolves, but you have survived with your integrity intact."

My father's words overwhelmed me, and I wondered if there were any truth in them. If I was a light within my family, it could only mean that God had been with me from the moment I was born, and I never knew it. A certain scripture that I had read had convinced me that God knows every person before they are born: *Before I formed you in the womb I knew you; before you were born I set you apart.* Jeremiah 1:5. He is an omniscient God who knows the future of every person, and He knows from the moment of birth whether a person will accept salvation or not. My only question at that moment was why God had allowed me to endure such a horrible childhood. "Thanks, Dad," I said. "I think you may have said something nice to me."

"I tried," my father said.

~

The talk with my father enlightened me about my position in the family, but it did not change their dysfunctional behaviors while they were staying with me. It was only a short matter of time before they were out of control with their drinking and fighting, and they ignored my pleas for them to stop. My weakness toward them was turning into strength and anger. How dare they bring such behaviors into my safety zone? None of them were looking for a job or doing anything to improve their situation. They brought their alcohol and drugs into my home, along with their fighting and foul language.

For two weeks, I allowed them to do these things while I looked to God for the strength to deal with them. While they ran rampant in my apartment, I stayed holed up in my bedroom praying and reading scripture. It would have been easy for me to succumb to my usual depression and remain in bed while my family took over my apartment, but after a lifetime of giving in to my family, I was unwilling to give into them this time. I knew that God was with me somewhere even if I did not feel Him, and I drew strength from that. I also had the support of my therapist, who thought that my family staying with me was terrible for my emotional health, and she encouraged me to get them out as soon as possible. I planned to have them leave as soon as my father's worker's compensation checks started arriving. The idea of standing up for myself caused me to feel great anxiety, but I knew that it was something I needed to do. I was no longer a child under their domination.

They had been staying with me for nearly a month when my father's checks finally started arriving. I waited for two days after that to see if they would make plans to leave as they had promised me they would do. By the third day, it was obvious that they had no intention of leaving—or even of offering me any financial restitution for staying with me. They assumed I was going to allow them to stay there free indefinitely, but any hope that I had of getting my life and myself straightened out rested on me getting them out.

Knowing that the time had come, I took one last look at scripture. *God is our refuge and strength, a very present help in trouble.* Psalm 46:1. I closed my eyes, took a deep breath, asked God to help me, then went out and approached my family. "You have been here for nearly a month," I told them in a shaky voice, and I hoped that they would not hear my knees knocking together. "Dad is getting his checks now, so you should be getting your own place now."

All three of them stared at me as if I were an alien from another planet, and none of them said anything.

I felt my resolve faltering, and I struggled to remain strong. "Getting your own place was the plan from the beginning," I reminded them.

Still, nobody said anything. They only continued to stare me down. My mother's eyes bore hard into mine until I grew uncomfortable and had to look away from her. "If my landlord finds out that you are staying here, I could be asked to leave," I said. "You keep drawing attention to yourselves with all of your noise and arguing."

My mother finally spoke. "I knew we could never rely on you," she spat. "Some child you are, throwing your own family out into the street."

I looked back at her incredulously. Had she forgotten the many times that she had thrown me out into the streets, even as a young child? "You should not have to be on the street now that Dad has some income," I said.

"How far do you think three people can get on that measly check?" she asked. "We would not be able to afford anything after we paid rent."

*You mean you will not be able to afford alcohol or drugs*, I thought sourly. "Dad's check is enough for you to afford one of those weekly kitchenettes," I said. "Or maybe you can get a studio apartment."

"Three people living in a studio apartment?" Donnie spoke up. "What about food?"

"You can go to food pantries like I had to do," I said.

My mother's face tightened along with the knots of anxiety in my stomach. I knew that I was going too far for her liking, but I could not stop myself. I wanted them out of my apartment, and away from me so badly I could practically taste it.

"Do you really expect us to go to food pantries?" Donnie asked. "How embarrassing."

I became frustrated. "Then I guess it is time for you or mom to get a job," I told him. "There is no reason why neither of you is working."

Now I had done it. I could see the fury on my mother's face, and I knew that she was angry that I was talking back to them. She was also drinking, which did not help matters any. She jumped to her feet and said between clenched teeth, "Don't you talk to us like that. You are nothing. Do you hear me? You're nothing but worthless."

My insides felt like jelly, but I stood my ground. My mother had already done so much emotional damage to me over the years that I knew she could not do too much more. "I just want you to get out and get your own place now," I said calmly. "I have let you stay here long enough, and you are all taking advantage of me."

My mother reached out and slapped me hard across the face. Tears sprang to my eyes, and I instinctively put my hand to my cheek. I wanted to hit her back, but I remembered God's commandment to honor thy mother and thy father. They did not deserve my honor, but they were still my parents. More importantly, I wanted to try my best to conduct myself in a manner that would be pleasing to God, so I held my burning cheek and forced myself to remain quiet. "I just want you to get out," I repeated. "You have been here long enough."

A slap was not enough for my mother. She grabbed a fist full of my hair and yanked it so hard that she pulled some of it out. "Do you have enough balls to try to kick us out of here?" she yelled. "Who do you think you are? You are nothing but a fat and ugly pig who will never amount to anything! I wish you were never born!"

At that moment, all of the years of abuse that I had endured from her exploded within me, and I did not care at that point if God wanted me to honor her. I just wanted her dead. I rushed to the kitchen and pulled open a drawer. Blindly I grabbed the first knife that I could find.

My mother had followed me to the kitchen. "So now you think you're going to kill me?" she taunted. "Let me see if you have the guts to do it!"

My entire body shook violently. I had my back to her, and I stood there, clutching the knife and imagining what she would look like with her throat sliced from ear to ear. I knew that if I turned around, I would forever silence her, and I would never have to hear her hurtful words again.

"Let me see you do it," my mother kept taunting. "You big and brave child of mine. Or I should say, you fat and ugly child of mine."

*Just do it,* a voice whispered in my head, but the voice was not coming from any of my alters. *She deserves to die! It will be worth spending the rest of your life in jail! Just go ahead and do it!*

I could not get my legs to turn around no matter how hard I tried. Thoughts of God filled my head, and I knew that no matter what she said or did to me, God would not want me to harm her. "Help me, God," I begged aloud.

"God shit you out of his ass!" my mother screamed, only she did not say it that nicely.

Slowly I put the knife back in the drawer and turned around to face her.

"I knew you did not have the guts," my mother said.

Beads of sweat formed on my forehead. "I do have the guts," I said. "God just saved your life, and He saved me from spending the rest of my life in jail. Now either you get out, or I am going to call the police and have them forcefully remove you."

"You try that," my mother said. "The cops will not make us get out of here tonight. Have you forgotten that I used to be a manager of an apartment building and that I know the laws? They will tell you that you have to give us thirty-day notice to vacate."

I did not know if that were true and I did not care. I was more interested in keeping myself from harming her like I still so wanted to do.

At that moment, Donnie came up from behind us and put his arm around my mother's shoulders. "Let's just leave," he told her. "This isn't worth it. It is not worth anybody getting hurt over when you know we can afford a kitchenette. Let's just grab some clothes, and then Dad and I can come get the rest of our stuff tomorrow."

My mother continued to glare at me. "I am not going to live in any kitchenette," she seethed.

"It's better than living in the car," Donnie said. "We really cannot stay here if Lisa does not want us here. Whether the cops allow us thirty days or not, we will still have to leave eventually."

"That is thirty more days that I can make her life hell here," my mom said.

"You have already had years of making my life hell," I breathed. "I am not going to let you do anymore. It is time for you to learn that you cannot go around doing whatever you want to whoever you want."

I saw Donnie tighten his grip on my mother's shoulders to prevent her from lunging at me again. I was sure that if she did not get out that night, one of us would end up killing the other. The hatred between us was all-consuming at that moment. "We will leave," Donnie said tiredly. "Come on mom, let's just go and end this."

"If we leave tonight this will never be over," my mother warned me. "You will be my enemy for the rest of your life."

"What would be any different about that?" I said. "Haven't I been your enemy since the day I was born?"

"You got that right," my mother said. "If you had not been born I would—"

I cut her off. "I know the story," I said. "If I hadn't been born you would not be stuck in a miserable marriage and an unhappy life. You would have made something good of yourself. You do not want to take any responsibility for any choices you made in your life. You would rather blame me for your choices. If that makes you feel better, you can keep blaming me for the rest of your life. You can do it somewhere else. Please just go."

My mother was too angry to take the time to gather any of her clothes. She headed for the door, but she stopped in the doorway and spat at my feet. "Wench," she hissed before she walked out to the car, slamming the door so hard behind her that the window next to do the door shook.

My brother and father took a few minutes to throw some of their clothes into garbage bags. My father made sure that he took the rest of the beer that was in the refrigerator. "We will come get the rest of our stuff tomorrow," Donnie said as they were leaving.

"I am sorry," I told him. "I love you, but I can't take this. You need to get away from them and try to get your own life together."

"Whatever," Donnie said with a wave of his hand. After.my family left, I collapsed in a heap onto the kitchen floor and sobbed hysterically for what seemed like hours. Every negative emotion that was possible for a human being to feel, I felt at that moment. Anger, fear, guilt, and despair overwhelmed me that night. God had spared my mother from my hand, and He had spared me from my mother's hand. After she had left, I cried out to Him for all that I was worth. I yelled at Him for allowing me to have the family that I had and the childhood that I had. It was not fair. I feared my mother's wrath that could come. I had never stood up to her like that and I had no idea what it would mean for my relationship with her. She could be very vindictive, and I did not doubt that she would do her best to make my life more difficult than it already was. I wondered if I had made a mistake by standing up for myself. I began to doubt my decision to make them leave. I felt guilty, especially about having thrown my brother out with them, but I knew that he was only taking advantage of me as well. For all of my life, I had felt like it was my responsibility to try to fix their problems. My mother had blamed me for her problems for so long that it was easy for me to blame myself. I knew that their life choices belonged solely to them, but my mother had spent years effectively burdening me with guilt about it. This was the first time I had ever forced them to be responsible for themselves, but instead of rejoicing about my strength, I was a quivering mess of fear and despair. I had spent most of my life doing my best to try to keep my mother from getting angry with me to avoid her wrath, and this time I had done the worst thing I could do to provoke her. I wanted to call her back and beg for her forgiveness, to beg her not to be angry with me, but I knew it was too late for that. What was done was done, and now I would have to face the possible repercussions of what I had done.

When my tears were spent I did the only thing I felt I could do at that moment: try to get some comfort from God. I felt so alone, and He was the only one that I had. I retrieved my Bible and began to search for some word from Him. I came across this scripture: *Though I walk in the midst of trouble, You will revive me; You will stretch out Your hand against the wrath of my enemies, and Your right hand will save me.* Psalm 138:7. I hoped against all hope that it was true, and that God would continue to protect me from my mother's fury.

I was frightened because I still felt an emotional disconnection from God the Father, so I had to put my blind trust in His words. I depended entirely on what Pastor Dave had told me about God. He had told me that God was incapable of telling a lie, and therefore I could take every promise in the Bible as truth. I was relying on the fact that because Jesus was my savior, I could trust in all of God's promises. It was difficult to trust those promises when I felt so insecure, but I had nothing else.

# Twelve

*Therefore, having been justified by faith, we have*
*peace with God through our Lord Jesus Christ.*
*(Romans 5:1)*

For several months after I had gotten my family out of my apartment, I heard not a word from them. My mother did not want anything more to do with me, and I knew that my father and Donnie were following suit to keep the peace with her. My other brother, Brian, had let me know that they were living in a small apartment in a neighboring town, but that was all that I knew. I was grateful for the silence so that I could work on the issues in my own life without any troublesome interference from them.

That silence from my family ended one warm summer day when my phone rang after I had just returned home from Sunday morning church service. I did not want to answer it, but I finally gave in to the persistent ringing. "Hello?"

There was a moment of silence, and I was just about to hang up when my mother's curt voice traveled from the other end of the line. "This is your mother," she said.

My heart flipped anxiously the second I heard my mother's voice. She did not sound friendly. I assumed that she was either drunk or high and that she was finally going to exact her wrath on me for having sent them out of my apartment months before. My mother was known for holding grudges for years. I fought to keep my voice from trembling as I responded to her. "Yes?" I asked.

"Hang up the phone," Little One urged me. She was talking to me silently in my head, and I tried to ignore the distraction.

"I am calling about your father," my mother said flatly. "He is dying."

I did not think that I heard her correctly. "I beg your pardon?" I said.

My mother's voice went from flat to impatient. "Do you have wax in your ears?" she asked. "Your father is dying. His doctor has informed us that he has terminal esophagus cancer. His prognosis is a year, maybe less."

I was too stunned to respond. My entire body went numb. I could not make sense out of what she was saying.

"Are you still there?" my mother snapped.

"No," I said. I felt like I was dissociating, but I was still conscious and still in control of my body. As my mother's words began to register, I dropped the phone and began to sob. My legs grew weak, and I blindly reached for something to grab. I stumbled toward the couch and sank into it.

I could hear Little One trying to talk to me, but it sounded as if she were a million miles away. I felt like I was drowning, and I wished I could grab onto her and hold her.

"Death is coming to all of us," Bug shrieked. "Death and decay are the punishments for our sins."

Bug's words only made me collapse into further hysteria. In addition to the devastation I felt knowing that I would soon lose my father, I was also terrified of what his death would mean for my mother. She was an emotionally dependent person who could not function on her own, and I could not stand the thought of her possibly having to live with me.

"Death comes to all mankind," Bug continued. "Blessed is the man who escapes the second death." I knew that Bug was frightened by my intense reaction, but I was unable to control my growing hysteria.

"Everybody calm down!" Little Lisa yelled.

"Lisa just received heartbreaking news," Little One said. "Let her cry if she wants to."

"Lisa is losing control of herself," Little Lisa warned. "If you want to let her lose control of herself, then you can clean up any messy behaviors that follow."

I struggled to control my tears, and eventually, my hysterical sobbing reduced to quiet hiccups. Suddenly I realized that my mother was still on the phone when I had dropped it. I rushed to pick up the phone, but she was no longer there. "I have to go there," I said. "I have to see my Dad."

"Give yourself some time to digest the news first," Little One suggested. "Waiting an hour or two is not going to make any difference."

I went back to the couch and put my head in my hands. I could not believe that my father was going to die at fifty-four years old. I knew that his impending death was going to change the relationship between my mother and me drastically, but I had no idea what that would mean for us.

~

Without any treatment, my father's health decline was swift. Within six months, his six-foot-one frame had whittled away to ninety-five pounds, and he became a shell of his former self. I spent as much time as I could with him, but our relationship remained awkward. I was not sure how to talk to him about what was happening to him. I approached his decline as though I were watching two airplanes on a collision course with each other. I could sense the destruction and pain that was inevitably coming, and I was powerless to stop it.

My mother could sense how much I was struggling with the situation, and she took every opportunity available to point out my failure. As my father's life on earth inched closer to its end, the flames of hatred in my heart toward my mother erupted into a burning inferno. If she cared that my father was dying, she did not show it. Instead, she continued to make our family life ripe with dissension. I hated her more, not only for having caused me so much emotional damage over the years but also for refusing to allow my father to die with peace and dignity. I felt angry with God for taking my father instead of my mother. How could God leave me with the one person that I despised so much?

I feared where my father was going to spend eternity after his death. Although my father had at times expressed a brief interest in God, I knew that he was not saved. I decided to try to talk to him about it. Tentatively I brought the subject of eternity up to him one day while I was at his apartment spending time with him. He was so thin and frail that it hurt me to look at him. His ribs jutted out from beneath his shirt, and I could see the outline of his spine when his back was to me. Uncertain of how to witness to him, I blurted out: "Dad, what do you think will happen to you after you pass away?"

"I don't care what happens to me," my father responded listlessly.

A little bit of discomfort squeezed my heart. "Do you believe that you will go somewhere after you die?" I asked.

My father looked at me with sunken eyes. "Does it matter?" he asked in return.

"Of course, it matters," I replied anxiously. "Don't you want to spend your eternity in heaven?"

My father gave me a blank look. He seemed too sick to care.

I heard a scoffing noise from my brother, who was sitting in a chair next to me. "There is no such thing as heaven or hell," he said.

"How do you know for sure?" I asked.

"I do not believe there is," Donnie said. "Look at Dad's condition and tell me there is a God."

I felt helpless. I was failing at my witnessing. I did not know why God allowed some people to suffer, so I was not quite sure how to respond. My mind fumbled as I tried to think of something appropriate from the Bible. "God has appointed man to die once for his sins," I said. "But blessed is the man who escapes the second death."

~

Donnie looked at me as though I were speaking a foreign language. Feeling desperate to make my point about the afterlife, I turned my

attention back to my father, who seemed to be rapidly giving up on our conversation. "If you would just tell God that you believe in Jesus, you will go to heaven," I said.

I instantly felt a prick in my spirit, and I knew that what I had just said was not entirely accurate. Just believing in Jesus would not be enough. It would make salvation a head issue instead of a heart issue, which was why I was struggling. I knew that to get into heaven, my father would first have to believe that he was a sinner in need of a Savior. How could I convince him of his need for a savior when I had trouble understanding it myself?

"Why do you keep coming over here preaching religion at us?" Donnie asked impatiently. "When are you going to understand that we do not want to hear it? If Mom comes out of her bedroom and hears you trying to preach to us again, you know what she will say to you."

I was disappointed in my inability to witness to my family. A feeling of failure settled over me as I stood there looking helplessly at my father. Once again, I was left feeling responsible for fixing my family, and I had still failed. I could not penetrate their hardened hearts toward God.

My father shifted restlessly in his chair. He seemed hesitant to say something to me. Finally, he said quietly, "Lisa, I am going to die."

A huge lump formed in my throat. I looked at the floor so that he would not see the tears in my eyes. "I know," I said. "I am sorry, Dad."

My father cleared his throat. "I am worried about your mother," he continued. "One of you is going to have to look after her."

I felt my heart quicken. "Donnie will be here with her," I reminded him.

When my father did not reply, I looked up at him. I could tell by the expression on his face that he did not believe Donnie was responsible enough to see after my mother. Donnie and my mother were both substance abusers. They would likely not bode well alone together.

"You know that I cannot do it," I said.

"Please make sure that your mother is okay," my father said. "I love her."

I did not know how my father could say that he loved my mother. After years of violence and dysfunction, I could not believe that he had any love

left at all for her—if he had ever really loved her in the first place. Whether he loved her or not, I had nothing but hate for her. I wanted nothing to do with looking after her. Still, I knew that I would lie to him, to try to give him some peace before he passed away. If my father were willing to believe that I would care for my mother after all of the emotional damage she had caused me, I would let him believe it.

Although I was willing to let my father believe that I would see after my mother, I was not going to allow my brother to believe it. I shot Donnie a warning look to let him know that my mother was going to be his responsibility after my father died. Donnie knew that my mother and I could not tolerate each other.

Donnie looked back at me sympathetic and apologetic eyes. I had never seen him look that way before. The look on his face startled me. "Is something wrong?" I asked.

Donnie slowly shook his head, but something going on with him that I could not quite put my finger on. His eyes were telling me something, but I had no idea what he was trying to say. After a few minutes, he looked away from me, and I decided to let it go.

I should never have let it go. I should have pursued that look that he gave me that day. I should have kept questioning him. I should have relentlessly pried into his thoughts until the meaning of that look became clear.

That look was a warning, and although the words remained unspoken, it was the last thing that my brother ever said to me.

# Thirteen

*No grave trouble will overtake the righteous, but
the wicked shall be filled with evil. (Proverbs 12:21)*

I received a phone call from my father early one December morning. He was clearly at the end of his time on this earth. His doctor estimated that he had a few weeks left; a couple of months at the very most. He rarely called me, so I knew that something was wrong the minute I heard his weakened voice. My heart sank before I knew why he was calling. I assumed he was calling to say that he felt it was his last day alive and to say goodbye to me.

"What is it, Dad?" I asked as I struggled to keep my rising emotions controlled.

My father's words were slow and deliberate. "Your brother Donnie passed away last night," he said. "I found him dead in his bed a couple of hours ago."

"My brother is gone?" I said.

"He is gone," my father confirmed. "It looks like he died from a drug overdose, but we won't know for sure until an autopsy is performed."

Darkness swallowed me whole. I could not see or hear anything else. I was trapped in a vast and airless sea of darkness that seemed to stretch forever. There were no doors or windows. I was terrified. I could not see. I could not breathe. I was certain that I was dead, but neither

God nor heaven was anywhere to be found. I could feel myself screaming, but there was nothing but silence.

I do not know how long I remained in that darkened state. It seemed like I was there for days, weeks, forever. At some point, I stopped screaming and collapsed into an exhausted heap.

The look on my brother's face the last time that I saw him loomed before me. I knew then what he had been trying to tell me through his eyes. Although Donnie had a better relationship with my mother than I had, the thought of being alone with her after my father passed away was too much for him. Death would be easier for him than being responsible for her. Without my father there as a buffer between them, Donnie knew that my mother would depend on him in every way that she could. Her constant needs and demands would have destroyed what little life he did have within him.

How I hated my mother at that moment—I thought she had surely killed my brother as if she had been the one to force the drugs into him!

From somewhere miles away I heard Little One calling my name. Her voice came to me in faint echoes, and then it began to assault my ears like booming thunder. A small beam of light cracked into the darkness, bringing wisps of cool air with it. I felt my body shudder as I began to gasp in the air. The crack of light began to grow larger until only a small slice of darkness remained.

I could see my alters standing beside me, two on each side of me. "Good heavens!" Little One exclaimed. "You fainted."

I kept gulping in air. I felt like I could not get enough of it into my lungs. "Is my brother dead?" I gasped.

"I am sorry, Lisa," Little One replied sadly. "He is dead."

I saw darkness begin to overtake the light again, threatening to swallow me forever. I closed my eyes and beckoned it to claim me.

"Stand up," Little Lisa demanded. "Stand on your feet, Lisa."

"I can't. I have no legs," I wailed. "My legs are gone."

"Your legs were blown off in the war," Bug yelled. "Our legs and arms are gone. We only have a torso and a head."

"That is not true." Little Lisa's voice sounded urgent. "Lisa, get on your feet. We cannot get the body up this time. You have to find the strength to do it yourself."

"Can't you see that I have no legs?" I screamed.

"Do not allow yourself be so weak," Little Lisa said. "Your legs are still there. Now get up and stand on them. Help us to get up. We are relying on you this time. We all need you now."

"My brother is dead," I wailed. "My father is almost dead. My mother is going to be my responsibility."

"This is too much for Lisa to deal with," Little One said. "Her brain is blowing circuits from the overload of stress she is feeling."

"I am trying to get her up," Little Lisa said. "I cannot seem to move the body this time."

"That is because Lisa runs us," Little One reminded her. "Lisa does not have even one ounce of strength within her that we can grab onto and help her."

Silence ensued for a few minutes. I could see that Mouse had turned herself away from all of us.

"What are you doing, Mouse?" Little One asked.

"I am ignoring this situation," Mouse replied.

"Can you help Lisa to stand up?" Little One asked.

Mouse considered it. "Will you try to kill yourself if I help you stand up?" she asked me.

"Yes," I said, for I knew that I would. I did not want to face what was happening to my family.

"Then I am not going to help you get up," Mouse said.

Mouse's light and carefree tone enraged me. "How can you still be happy when I just found out that my brother is dead, and my dad is soon going to die?" I yelled. "How can you be so disrespectful towards my family and me?"

Mouse became serious, which was a rare aura for her. "Don't you know that life and death are connected through God?" she asked.

God was the last thing I wanted to hear about at that moment. He had crushed my fragile faith and trust in Him by allowing this to happen to me. The idea that God would not give a Christian more than he or she could bear was not true. I was lying flat on my back with the weight of the world crushing me.

Mouse knew my thoughts. "God is here with you," she assured me. "He will help you through this if you ask Him to."

"If this is how God helps people then I don't want His help," I said.

"Why can't you feel the connection that I feel?" Mouse asked. "Why can't you feel that everything in this world is connected through God? All of the people in this world are connected whether they are alive or dead. The sky, the grass, the houses, the cars, everything in this world is connected. Everything belongs to God. God owns everything and everybody in this world. Everything is one through our Lord."

I thought Mouse was crazy, and I did not want to hear any more of her outlandish ideas about God. I just wanted to close my eyes and have life disappear. I did not have the strength nor the desire to face what was happening to me.

Little Lisa soon grew tired of my inability to get up off the floor. Using all of her effort, she finally managed to heave my body into a standing position. I felt heavy, as if my body were encased in cement.

"Ask God to help you," Mouse encouraged.

"God can leave me alone," I spat. "How can a God who is supposed to be so loving do this to me?"

"God is not doing this to you," Mouse said. "Your family has done this to themselves. It is not God's fault that your brother became a drug addict. It is not God's fault that your father's propensity for heavy drinking and smoking could have led to his esophagus cancer. God loves people enough to allow them to have free will over their lives. It is not fair to blame God for the choices that people make. It is also not God's fault that you and your mother have such a horrible relationship. However, He loves you, and He wants to help you deal with the ways that the choices other people make affect you."

~

If it were not for my alters, I might not have gone to my brother's funeral. I did not want to see his body lying in the casket, and I did not want to see my mother, whom I was still convinced had killed him.

On the day of Donnie's funeral, I was too depressed to get out of bed. Not only was I still angry with my mother, but I was also angry with God. Although Mouse kept telling me that God never promises us a fair life, I was somewhat disillusioned with God by that point. I still had the idea that once a person confessed Jesus as their Savior, God would make that person's life better. I compared myself with the many mega preachers that I saw on television. God seemed to be making their lives easy. Why could those people have million-dollar homes and good lives, while I was losing my family, struggling financially, and was still suffering from mental illness? It was not fair. God played favorites. Either that or I was the worthless person that my mother kept telling me I was. I could not seem to do enough to win God's favor. I was only getting hard luck from Him.

"Stop feeling sorry for yourself and get up," Little Lisa told me in her usual impatient way. "You will never forgive yourself if you miss your brother's funeral."

I pulled the blanket over my head. The shock still had not worn off that I had lost my brother and was about to lose my father. I felt an enormous lack of control over my life, and it was terrifying.

Little Lisa took the blanket and tossed it on the floor. "If you do not get up, I will get you up," she warned.

"We will help you get through this," Little One assured me. I could always count on Little One to give me strength.

I leaned on Little One's strength as I walked into the funeral home. The moment that I walked through the door smelling of stale cool air filled my nostrils. It was that scent of death that so many funeral homes have. Family and friends immediately surrounded me and murmured well-meaning words of sympathy. I brushed past them and walked into the viewing room.

I walked slowly up to the casket and looked down at my brother. He was dressed in his favorite cap and baseball shirt. Somebody had placed a single white rose in his clasped hands. Tears fell from my lowered head onto his shirt. *I am so sorry* I told my brother silently. *I did not know she was killing you, too. I did not realize that it was so difficult for you.*

"Come away from the casket and sit down," Little One encouraged. She could feel the sorrow ripping through my heart, and she was concerned for me.

I turned and scanned the crowd that was sitting in the chairs on the other side of the room. My parents were sitting in the front row. My father looked as if he might collapse at any moment. He was very weak, just a whisper of the man that he had been a year before. My mother sat next to him, stone-faced and rigid, her eyes staring blankly at her dead son. I could not tell if she was feeling any emotion. I did not care.

I made my way over to my father and placed my hand on his bony shoulder. I bent toward his ear and whispered, "Are you doing okay, Dad?" I asked.

My father nodded and placed his arm around my mother.

"I am going to sit in the back until the service starts," I told him.

My father nodded again. I glanced at my mother. I could not bring myself to acknowledge any emotion that she might be feeling. She turned her head and gave me a hard look. I knew that she wished it were me in that casket instead of my brother.

I made my way to the last row of chairs and sat huddled in a corner. I hoped that everybody would leave me alone. I did not want to talk to anybody. I was on the verge of breaking down into hysteria at any second.

"There are no religious items in here," Mouse said. I appreciated that she was talking inside of my head so that nobody else in the room would hear her.

I looked around the room. There were no indications of God or Jesus anywhere.

"Must be a non-denominational funeral home," Little Lisa remarked.

"Is there such a thing?" Little One asked.

In my mind, I could see Bug with her eyes tightly closed. She was afraid of dead bodies and funeral homes. She was afraid of many things. I knew that her fears came directly from me.

"I think that some funerals are held in churches," Little One mused.

"It probably depends on if the person who died was religious," Little Lisa said.

I stopped listening to their chatter when the service began. I made my way back up to the front and sat next to my father during the service. My other brother, Brian, sat next to my mother. I noticed that my mother was clinging onto Brian's hand so hard that her knuckles were white, but her face was still stony. My father leaned against my shoulder, and quiet sobs wracked his thin body. I placed my hand gently on his arm. We were together, yet we were alone with our pain and sorrow.

Donnie's service was simple and short. I held my father's body up, while Little One held my body up. It disturbed me that the service was a non-religious service. Donnie was an atheist, but I did not want God eliminated from his death. I had a little flicker of hope that my brother had called out to God and professed Jesus as his savior as he was near death. It was unlikely, but still possible.

~

After the service, my parents, Brian and I lined up at the casket to say our final goodbyes to Donnie. As I looked down at my brother, I quietly began to pray what I could remember of the 23rd Psalm. I wanted something—*anything*—of God buried with my brother. When I finished praying, I looked up to find my mother glaring at me. Her eyes were as hard as diamonds. "Leave him alone," she hissed quietly through her clenched teeth. "Do not start your preaching here."

I wanted to scream at her, to tell her that she had caused Donnie's death as much as the drugs that he had taken had caused it. I wanted to physically attack her and make her feel the pain that I was feeling. However, Little

One was there within me, comforting and calming me, and helping me to stay in control of myself. I was grateful for Little One's help then because, without her, there would have been a violent scene next to my brother's casket. It was one of the more frequent occurrences when I was finding out that there was some benefit to having alters.

Turning away from my mother, I relinquished control of my body to Little One and let her walk out of the funeral home. There was going to be a luncheon after the service that I was expected to attend, but I had reached my maximum capacity for functioning that day. I wanted Little One to attend the luncheon in my place, but her voice was different than mine, which would be noticed by my friends and family. Each of my alters had their own distinct way of talking, and none of their voices matched mine.

"You go to the luncheon, and we will hold you up like we did at the funeral," Little One assured me.

"I do not know if I can stand being around my mother for even five more minutes," I said wearily.

"God will help us to help you," Little One said.

"I am still angry with God about all of this," I admitted.

"Angry or not, God still loves you," Little One said. I was not so sure about God's love for me at that moment. My brother was on his way to his grave, and my father would be on the way to his grave very soon. The fate of my relationship with my mother was uncertain, and the fear of having to be the one to take care of her caused me to feel as if no air was getting into my lungs.

# Fourteen

*For if you forgive men their trespasses, your heavenly Father will also forgive you. But if you do not forgive men their trespasses, neither will your Father forgive your trespasses. (Matthew 6:14-15)*

My father passed away three months after my brother did, leaving the dilemma of what to do with my mother. She did not work, did not drive a car, and had never lived on her own. She was a substance abuser and did not have the emotional maturity or desire to continue living on her own. She had been dependent on my father in almost every way for her entire adult life.

Eventually, it was decided that my mother would live with my brother Brian. He did not want to take her in, but he had a better relationship with her than I did. When Brian agreed to take her in, I collapsed with relief and gratitude. After years of living apart from my mother, I knew that neither she nor I would have been able to tolerate being together again. We hated each other too much.

If my mother cared at all about my father's death, her grief was eclipsed by the death of her son. Donnie was the only child out of the three of us that she had any real fondness for, and she took his death hard. After she moved in with Brian, her substance abuse escalated. Whenever she would see me, she would scream that I should have died instead of my brother. Her words wounded me, so I tried to stay away from Brian's house as much as possible.

She made it clear that she did not want me around. Being in my presence only increased her anger over my being alive while Donnie was not.

Adjusting to the losses in my family was difficult for me, mainly because I knew that neither my father nor my brother was in the right standing with God when they died. I was haunted by the thought of them spending eternity in hell. Whenever a well-meaning person would tell me that my father and brother were resting peacefully in a better place, I cringed because I knew that it probably was not true. Not everybody who dies automatically goes to a better place.

I consoled myself by thinking that perhaps God would be merciful to my father and Donnie. After all, they were not bad people. They had not lived perfect lives, but surely, they had not been bad enough to deserve hell.

Mouse would not allow me to lie to myself about it. "The Bible is clear in saying that no man can get to God except through Jesus," she reminded me. "It does not matter how good of a life a person lives. Jesus is the only way to heaven."

"That just proves that God is mean," I replied.

"How is that mean?" Mouse challenged. "God made one way to heaven, and He gives every person free will to decide whether they want to accept that way or not. That doesn't sound mean to me."

"A loving God should not send people to hell," I protested.

"God does not send people to hell. People send themselves to hell if they decide not to accept Jesus as their Savior," Mouse said. She paused and then added, "Lisa, I do not think that you are saved like you think you are."

"How can you say that?" I asked angrily. "I accepted Jesus as my Savior years ago!"

"You accepted Jesus in your head but not in your heart," Mouse replied. "You accepted Jesus because you wanted God to help you get away from your family. You had a motive for accepting Jesus. I don't think you know what salvation means."

"Don't be ridiculous. Of course, I am saved," I said. "I pray, don't I? I used to clean the church for Sunday services. I have been to Bible studies. I go to church on Sunday. How can I not be saved?"

Mouse shook her head. "You do not know God or what He has done for you," she insisted. "You are living the motions, but not the real experience."

Little One could feel my anger rising, and she joined the conversation to try to smooth it over. "What Mouse is saying is that you still have a skewed concept of God," she explained. "You still see God and Jesus as separate, and you still view God as mean and punishing. Your faith and trust in God are low, and you have doubts that God truly loves you because you see yourself as an unworthy person."

What Little One said was accurate, and shame began to creep into my heart. My relationship with God was sorely lacking, but did that mean that I was not saved?

"In your head, you think you love Jesus," Mouse said. "But do you love Him in your heart?"

Mouse had me feeling flustered. "I don't know much about love," I admitted. "But I do know that Jesus died for me."

"But you do not know what it means that Jesus died for your sins," Mouse said. "You do not think that Jesus should have had to die for you."

"I get tired of being called bad," I sighed.

"You think God sees you the same way that your mother sees you," Mouse said. "You cannot accept God's love because your mother has caused you to believe that you are an unworthy and unlovable person. You think if your mother cannot love you, then how could the God of the universe possibly love you?"

I felt trapped by the truths that were difficult to face. "You are hurting me, Mouse," I said. "Leave me alone. You are not my therapist."

"I know more about you than your therapist does," Mouse said. "What I am saying also ties in with why you dislike Little Lisa so much. She is all the parts of you that your mother hates, and that has caused you to hate yourself."

"You can talk about all of this psychological mess until you are blue in the face, but it will not change anything," I said. "I am too far gone."

"Not true," Mouse said. "God showed me the way that you can learn to have the right relationship with both Him and Little Lisa."

Curiosity got the best of me. "Is there a certain Bible study I should go to?" I asked.

"No," Mouse said. "The way to begin fixing your relationship with God and with yourself is to start by forgiving your mother for all that she has done to damage your heart."

My reaction to that was swift and intense. The idea of forgiving my mother was repulsive to me. "My mother does not deserve my forgiveness," I declared. "Two people could not hate each other more."

"Do you deserve God's forgiveness?" Mouse asked. "Yet He forgave you before you were even born."

"That is different," I protested. "I have not done the things to God that are as wrong and as bad as my mother has done to me."

Mouse let out a gasp. "The sins that you have committed were bad enough that God allowed His son to die for them," she said.

"There it is again," I said. "Everything that has to do with my relationship with God only points out how bad I am."

"But more than that, it points out God's love for you," Mouse said.

"I think I am going to give up on God," I said quietly. "Ever since I claimed Jesus as my Savior, my life has only gotten worse. I lost my job, I lost my brother and my father, and now you are telling me I will have to forgive my mother before I can feel God's love for me. God is asking too much of me if He expects me to forgive a person who has done so much damage to me. It's because of my mother that I lost my entire childhood and that I now struggle with so many emotional issues."

"And it is because of you that Jesus was beaten and put to death on the cross," Mouse said gently.

"Don't say that!" I cried out. "I am not the one who crucified Jesus. That happened two thousand years before I was born. Perhaps if God had

sent Jesus to earth during this day and age, He would not have had to die as He did." My shoulders slumped from the discouragement I felt. "I don't know why God has to be so displeased with me," I moaned. "It is not like I go around hurting other people or doing bad things like that."

Mouse seemed thoughtful. "You have lied during your life," she said.

"Everybody tells a white lie now and then," I said.

"You have stolen during your life," Mouse continued.

"I am no thief!" I protested.

"What about that lip gloss that you stole from Walgreens when you were nine years old?" Mouse challenged.

I felt my face grow red with shame. "One of your personalities must have done that," I said weakly.

"Do not blame us!" Bug shrieked anxiously. "You are the one who stole that lip gloss."

"I was a child," I said. "My cousin dared me to take it."

"Even so, stealing is a sin against God," Mouse said.

"God would condemn me for finger lifting a sixty-nine-cent tube of lip gloss?" I asked incredulously.

"Was it right to take that lip gloss without paying for it?" Mouse asked.

"Would God send me to hell for *that*?" I replied. It hurt my heart to think that God would hold against me what I considered such a minor infraction.

"There are two points here," Mouse said. "The first point is that every human is born with the tendency toward sinning. The second point is that God is so holy, He cannot stand even your theft of lip gloss." Mouse paused and then sighed. I could sense that she was frustrated with my lack of comprehension about sin. "It is not that God is watching every little move you make, waiting to punish you for it," she continued. "It is that God cannot stand any kind of sin because of how good He is. It is His character. Sin separates you from God, but He does not want to condemn you for your sins. Jesus said He came to the world to save people, not to condemn them. God wants to forgive you for your sins. That is why He allowed His son to come to this earth and die for you."

"I know this," I said impatiently. "How many times are you going to tell me this?"

"Until you understand your need for a Savior," Mouse replied.

"I understood it a long time ago," I said.

"Nope," Mouse said stubbornly.

"What do you mean by that?" I asked.

"You may have told God from your head that you need a Savior, but you did not tell Him that from your heart," Mouse said. "You were trying to get in good standing with God by playing by the rules, but your heart is still full of bitterness and hate."

"I am certain that God understands why I hate my mother," I said. "He knows what she has done to me. He would not expect me to forgive her after the emotional damage she has caused me. I think He would give me a reprieve against forgiveness this time."

"Really?" Not to be deterred, Mouse picked up my Bible from the table and began to thumb through it.

"You show me where God says I should forgive my mother," I said smugly.

"Right here," Mouse said. "In 1 John 4:20 it says, *'If someone says I love God but hates their brother, he is a liar; for he who does not love his brother whom he has seen, how can he love God whom he has not seen?'"*

"That does not say I have to forgive my mother," I said.

Mouse flipped through several more pages and then said, "Matthew 6:14-15 says, *'For if you forgive men their trespasses, your heavenly Father will also forgive you. But if you do not forgive men their trespasses, neither will your Father forgive you.'"*

I looked at the page to where Mouse was pointing to see if God actually said that. It was there in the Bible, as clear as day. I could not argue that point with Mouse. "That makes me so uncomfortable," I said.

Mouse closed the Bible and placed it back on the table. "Of course, it does," she says. "You do not see your own need for God's forgiveness yet."

Once again, I found myself feeling angry with God. How could He compare my mother's physical and emotional abuse with my stealing a tube of lip gloss as a child? How could those sins be equal in His eyes? Why was He expecting me to forgive my mother, without expecting her to beg for my forgiveness first? "My mother's sins were worse than my sins," I told Mouse.

"All sins are equal to God, no matter how big or how small they are," Mouse replied.

"How is that fair?" I demanded. "Do you think God is fair to me?"

Mouse hesitated, weighing her words carefully. "You should be grateful that God is so fair and just," she said. "He allowed His son to die for your theft of that lip gloss as much as for your mother's abuse."

"But that is not—" I stopped short as Mouse's point began to register in my head.

"God is always fair," Mouse said quietly. "He does not play favorites. A sin is a sin to God. We are all accountable for our own sins. We all need God to forgive us."

"Maybe not you," I remarked. "You are just a personality. You are not a real person. Technically, you are just a psychological disorder. I guess that means you do not need God's forgiveness."

"I am a part of you," Mouse pointed out.

"I do not think Jesus died for personalities," I mused.

"What I know is that I am a part of you and if you need Jesus, then I need Him too," Mouse said. "I *want* Him to be my Savior."

"I don't know if I can forgive my mother," I said.

"Not on your own," Mouse said. "You will not be able to do it on your own. But besides the scriptures that I just read to you, there is something else significant in the Bible."

"What is that?" I asked.

"It says with God, nothing is impossible," Mouse replied.

# Fifteen

*In righteousness you shall be established; you shall
be far from oppression, for you shall not fear; and
from terror, for it shall not come near you.
(Isaiah 54:14)*

A few months after my mother moved in with my brother, he called to tell me that he needed me to start helping her with some things. "You know that I have to work during the day," he stated. "Mom needs rides to her medical appointments and other errands. See if you can help her with getting her laundry done and taking a shower. She does not want to lift a finger to help herself."

"She is just lazy," I retorted. "There is no reason that she cannot do her laundry or take a shower. She is used to Dad doing everything for her."

"I know that," Brian sighed. "But I am not Dad, and I am not going to wait on her hand and foot as he did. This living arrangement with her is getting on my nerves. If you do not want me to ship her over to live with you, then you will have to come by here sometimes and help her. I know that you two do not get along, but it is not fair for me to have to shoulder the burden by myself. I do have a life too, you know."

I knew that Brian was right, but the idea of helping my mother with anything was offensive to me. She had neglected me in every way when I was a child, and I thought that turnabout was fair play when it came to ignoring her needs. She was capable of meeting her own needs, other than driving herself to appointments. It made me angry that she was such a dependent person when I saw no need for it. However, my reluctance to help my mother paled in comparison to the terror that I felt about having her live with me, so I agreed to start going over to his house twice a week to see what I could do for her.

I forced myself to go to Brian's house the next day. Brian was at work, and I found my mother sitting at the kitchen table drinking beer. Her hair was dirty, and her clothes looked as if she had been wearing them for several days. "What are you doing here?" she demanded rudely.

I swallowed the dread and anxiety that being in her presence always produced within me. "Brian asked me to come by and help you with a few things," I replied.

"Help me with what?" she asked. "I don't need your help with anything."

I gestured toward her hair. "When was the last time that you took a shower?" I asked.

"That is none of your business," my mother snapped. "Go back home and take your own shower."

I took off my jacket and tossed it onto an empty kitchen chair. "Where is your dirty laundry?" I asked. "I will do that for you while you take a shower."

My mother took a long swallow of her beer and slammed it on the table. "I am not going to take a shower, and I can do my laundry," she said. "I do not want you here."

I was tempted to walk out and return home, but the threat of her moving in with me loomed large in my head. I looked around the messy kitchen and sighed. "Have you eaten?" I asked.

My mother gave me a defiant look. "I'm not hungry," she snapped.

I began to pick up the dirty dishes and load them into the dishwasher. "Why can't you help Brian keep this house clean?" I asked sourly. "He works all day, and you are sitting here doing nothing. You could at least clean up this kitchen."

My mother's eyes were like shooting daggers meant to kill me. "Don't worry about Brian and me," she said. "It is none of your business."

"Brian made it my business when he asked me to help you," I said. I opened the refrigerator and eyed what food was in there. "Would you like me to make you a bologna sandwich?" I asked. "I remember you once said that bologna goes well with beer."

"I can make my sandwich," she replied.

"You can but you won't," I said. I tried to keep the anger I was feeling from showing in my voice. When she did not respond, I made her a sandwich and set it on the table in front of her.

"You can eat that yourself," my mother said as she pushed the plate toward me. "You know I do not eat this early."

"It's noon," I said.

"You know I do not eat until evening," she said.

"Save it for later then," I sighed. "I am going upstairs to get your laundry together."

I expected her to protest, but she said nothing as I made my way up the stairs to her bedroom. I surveyed the mounds of clothes that were scattered on her bedroom floor. Not knowing which clothes were dirty, I gathered them all together and threw them into the washing machine. When I returned to my mother, I noticed that the sandwich I had made for her was gone. I suspected she had thrown it into the garbage. "Will you please take a shower?" I asked.

My mother fingered her empty beer can. "Why?" she asked in return.

"It looks as if you need one," I said.

My mother took a deep breath and heaved out a long sigh. "I will take one when the washing machine is finished," she said. "The water will run cold if I take one while the machine is going."

I was surprised by her lack of protest. I moved my jacket off the kitchen chair and sat down beside her.

My mother's eyes searched mine and then flickered away. "Don't get too comfortable in that chair," she warned, but her voice had lost some of its edge. "I do not want you here."

"I know that," I said. "And I don't want to be here, but Brian asked me to come."

"Since when do you listen to your brother?" my mother asked sarcastically.

I did not tell her about Brian's threat to have her live with me. "I told him that I would come by twice a week to help you out," I shrugged.

My mother looked surprised and then quickly tried to cover it.

"I know you hate me," I said quietly. "Let's try to make our time together as pain-free as possible."

My mother and I did not talk much more after that. I busied myself with her laundry and cleaned up the house. My mother took a shower after the laundry was finished, and I was relieved that Brian would come home to find everything in order, at least for that day.

"I'm leaving," I told my mother after I had been there for three hours. "I will be back in a few days."

"You can come back on Friday," my mother said. "I have a doctor's appointment that day. He will not renew my pain pills until I see him."

"What time do you have to be there?" I asked.

"One o'clock," my mother replied.

"I will be here at twelve-thirty," I sighed. I put on my jacket and began to head for the door.

"Lisa," my mother said.

I turned around and gave her an impatient look. "What is it now?" I asked.

My mother looked uncomfortable. "I guess I should say thank you," she said. "For doing my laundry and cleaning up the house."

I could not remember a time when my mother had ever thanked me for anything. It was as awkward for me as it was for her. "You are welcome," I mumbled, and then I escaped to the safety of my car.

As soon as I got into my car, I put my head on the steering wheel and began to cry. I was relieved to be away from my mother, but her attempt to show gratitude had touched my heart in some small way.

"You did well with her today," Little One whispered to me. "I am proud of you."

"God is proud of you too," Mouse said brightly.

"He is?" I asked hopefully. I wanted God to feel proud of me, even if I did not feel or understand His love for me.

"He told me so Himself," Mouse said confidently. "He spoke right to my heart and told me to tell you how proud He is that you helped your mother today."

I lifted my head and wiped the tears from my cheeks. "It was difficult for me," I admitted.

"But you did it," Little One said.

"I still hate her," I said. "Nothing has changed."

Suddenly I realized that I was still sitting in Brian's driveway. I looked at his house and saw that my mother was watching me through the living room window. I was not sure, but I thought I saw her hand slowly wave at me. I did not respond to her wave. I was not going to give her any more of myself that day.

~

On Friday, I picked up my mother for her doctor's appointment. I knew she would be ready because she was addicted to her pain pills and would not miss the opportunity to get them filled. There was not much conversation between us on the way there. The silence hung over me like a thick blanket, threatening to smother me with its awkward darkness. My mother and I did not know how to have a decent conversation with each other. Our efforts to talk through our disdain for one another were laced with contempt and unease.

My mother did not allow me to go into the doctor's office with her, but as we were getting back into the car afterward, I noticed how thin and frail she was. She could not have weighed more than ninety pounds soaking wet. A sliver of concern rose from somewhere deep in my heart. I pushed that concern away because it was unfamiliar and uncomfortable to me. "Would you like to stop and get something to eat?" I asked.

"I never feel hungry," my mother replied.

"Haven't you been eating? You look very thin," I remarked.

"How can I eat when my husband and my son are dead?" my mother blurted out.

I was too stunned to respond. It had not occurred to me that my mother was still struggling with grief and probably depression. She did not have any close friends, and she did not have many people to talk to. She was an island all to herself. For one quick moment, I was able to look past my hatred to see that despite her faults, she was still a human being who was suffering. I did not want to know that about her. I did not have a clue how to make her feel better. I was inadequate, and I was the last person in the world that she would want to try to console her. I fumbled for something to say but could find no words of meaning.

My mother did not seem to notice my lack of response. I was stunned again by the next words that came from her mouth. "Your brother did not believe in God, so what happened to him after he died?" she asked. "You believe in God. You tell me what happened to my son."

I pulled into Brian's driveway and turned to look at her. Our eyes met, and her eyes, usually so hard, were filled with pain and concern. "I do not know what happened to him," I replied quietly. I had my own distress over my brother's soul.

"You're supposed to know," my mother said in an accusing tone.

"What do you think happened to him?" I asked.

My mother looked away from me. She clasped her hands onto her lap and said, "I like to think that he is happy in heaven."

*God help me*, I thought. *I do not know how to talk to her about this.* How could I tell my grieving mother what the Bible warns about dying without Jesus? I felt that it was important not to deceive her with a lie, but I knew that telling her the biblical truth at that moment would destroy her.

"God says to ask her to go to church with you," Mouse said in my head.

It was the most absurd thing anybody could have ever suggested to me, but I was grasping at nothing at that moment. "Would you like to go to church with me on Sunday?" I blurted out.

My mother looked at me with disbelief. "Church?" she said. "I don't go to church. Why would I go to church?"

I was still fumbling for words. Inside of my head, Mouse was encouraging me on. "Maybe we can find out what happened to Donnie together if we go to church," I said.

"You go to church and find the answer for me," my mother said. "I do not belong in church."

"Everybody belongs in church," I said.

My mother shook her head. "I drink, cuss, and smoke," she said. "I am not going to stop doing any of that to go to church."

"God will accept you as you are," I said. "The first step is to come."

I heard Little Lisa say sarcastically, "You're a good one to tell her that God will accept her as she is when you don't believe it yourself. You should walk what you talk."

"Shut your mouth," I hissed at Little Lisa. It was difficult for me to focus on people externally when there were so many conversations always going on inside of my head.

"Did you just tell me to shut my mouth?" my mother asked angrily.

I realized that I had spoken to Little Lisa aloud instead of inside of my head. "I was not talking to you. I was thinking out loud," I said.

"You should shut your mouth because you will never convince me to go to church," my mother said.

I felt like I was not going to get anywhere with her about it at that moment, so I decided to drop the subject. I was disappointed. I wanted her to go to cop out of having to witness to her. If she was going to learn that not everybody goes to heaven when they die, I preferred that she learned it from my pastor rather than from myself.

As if my mother could read my mind, she fumbled in her pocket for a cigarette and then said slowly, "Besides, I've been around the block a few times during my life. Your Grandparents were Catholic."

"Do Catholics believe in hell?" I asked.

My mother lit her cigarette and took a long drag. I did not want her to smoke in my car, but I decided that our topic of conversation was more important than arguing over her smoking. "They believe in purgatory," she breathed. "That's where the dead go to be cleansed from their sins before they can get into heaven."

"There is nothing about purgatory in the Holy Bible," Mouse warned me.

My mother took another drag from her cigarette. "But I think when you are dead, you are dead," she said. "You're just gone."

"I used to think that way too," I said. "It is probably comforting for some people to think that way, but it is not true."

My mother had reached her limit for talking. "I am not going to sit in this car all day," she said. "I have had enough. I am tired."

"Do you realize that this was probably the longest decent conversation we have ever had together?" I asked. "We talked without arguing."

My mother gave me a strange look.

"Miracles do happen," Mouse crowed.

At that moment, it was difficult to doubt Mouse.

# Sixteen

*Let the word of Christ dwell in you richly in all*
*wisdom, teaching and admonishing one another in*
*psalms and hymns and spiritual songs, singing with*
*grace in your hearts to the Lord. (Colossians 3:16)*

At this time in my life, I began to feel dissatisfied with the church that I was attending. I had been going to the same church for years, and it had served its purpose for me, but the leadership had changed. Pastor Dave and Sue had moved away to another state the year before, and the new leadership family was doing things differently. The sermons were no longer moving my spirit, and I began to feel as though I were moving away from God rather than moving closer to Him. I knew that the answer was for me to find a different church for worship. It was a difficult decision for me to make because I was not a person who liked change, but my spiritual growth depended on it.

For the remainder of that year, I bounced around to different churches in the area, trying to find one that would light my spiritual fire again. I was disappointed as I went away from each church with the feeling that it was not the right one for me. I was praying for God to direct me to the church that He thought would be best for me, but He did not seem to be answering my prayer. I began to wonder if He was listening to my prayer. I was not used to God making me wait for answers to my prayers. I was an impatient person, and if He did not answer my prayers quick enough to suit me, I would then accuse Him of not hearing me and try to figure out a solution by myself. Waiting for answers to prayers have never been one of my strong points, and to this day God is often giving me lessons about my patience issue. After about four months of fruitless searching, I told God I was going to throw in the towel. "I give up," I told Him. "There isn't another church around here that is right for me. It looks like you do not want me to go to church anymore."

The day that I had given up on finding a church, I went to the grocery store for a few items. While I was waiting in the checkout line, my eye caught a big bold sign tacked onto the store bulletin board. It said, "Need a church home? South Point Christian Church meets every Sunday morning at 10:00 am in the Morris High School gymnasium. We would love for you to join us!"

*What kind of church meets in a high school gym?* I wondered, but I quickly forgot about it as I checked out and headed home. That evening as I was flipping through cable channels on television, there was the same church being advertised again—this time on the local community channel. My curiosity was piqued again. "God, are you trying to tell me that you want me to go to this church?" I prayed. "That can't be a real church."

God's only reply to me was a stirring in my heart that I attributed to the Holy Spirit encouraging me to go there on Sunday and check it out.

~

The South Point Christian Church looked the least like a church than anything I had ever seen. It had folding chairs and a podium in front of them. A man was sitting behind a set of drums and another man quietly strumming a guitar. Crowded with people of various ages, it looked more like people attending an athletic event rather than people gathering to worship the Lord. I stood in the back of the gym and looked around in disbelief. Was this where God wanted me to worship Him? Why were these people praising the Lord in a school gymnasium anyway? Something did not feel right to me, and I began to argue with God in my head. Surely, it could not have been Him leading me to such a place to worship. I could

not feel spiritual worshipping God in a school gym. I could not possibly worship in a room that had a basketball court on one end and locker rooms on the other end. I could not sit in battered folding chairs and listen to somebody talk about God in a place where high school kids gathered to do athletics. It did not seem spiritual in any way.

Thinking I had made a mistake in going there, I tried to make a beeline for the exit. An older man with a ruddy complexion and a broad smile stopped me. "Welcome!" he boomed. He held out one hand to me to greet me while handing me a bulletin that he had in his other hand.

I felt embarrassed that I was trying to slip out the door to leave. I shook his hand, took the bulletin, and gave him a faltering smile.

"I'm Pastor Dennis," the man went on. "We're glad to have you with us today."

My disbelief grew as I looked Pastor Dennis up and down. He looked like a pleasant man, but he did not look like a pastor. He wore jeans with a yellow T-Shirt that had the words *South Point Christian Church* blazed across the front. "It's nice to meet you," I said. He did not look like a pastor, but he did look like he fit right in with the rest of this so-called *church*.

"I hope you enjoy our service today," Pastor Dennis said as he moved away to greet other people who were waiting to talk to him. "The bulletin tells a little bit about our church, but please let me know if you have any questions."

A thick crowd had gathered in front of the door. Instead of leaving, I turned and sat in one of the folding chairs in the last row. The chair was hard and uncomfortable. I opened the program and glanced through it, pausing to greet the people who passed me by as they took their seats. On the back page of the bulletin, I found some brief information about the church. I learned that they were meeting in the school gymnasium only while they were waiting for a building to be built to accommodate their growing needs. The small building they were previously in no longer met their growing congregation, so they were meeting at the school for the next few months until a bigger building was completed. I was immediately relieved when I read that, and I was ashamed that I had judged their situation so harshly before I knew the facts. I decided that if the church was growing so rapidly that they needed a bigger building then perhaps I should give them a chance to see what they were all about. I decided to stay for the service.

While I was waiting for the service to begin, I carefully studied the page where they shared their beliefs. My spirit jumped when I read that they believed Jesus is the son of the living God, and that He is the author of our salvation. Their beliefs matched right up with mine, and I felt much more comfortable with being there. I closed my eyes and said humbly, "Forgive me for jumping to conclusions about these people, Lord. I am willing to give this a chance. If this is where you want me to be, please open my heart and my mind to know your will."

That was all that I needed to say to God to open up the floodgates of my soul. When the music started, my spirit was drawn to worship in a way that I had never felt before, not even in the previous church that I had attended for years. The music at this church was more modern, with more of a rock music edge to it, and I loved it. It uplifted my spirit tremendously. When Pastor Dennis stood up behind the podium and gave a sermon about trusting God in all circumstances, I hung on every word he spoke. I never felt closer to God than I did at that service in that high school gymnasium that day. I was disappointed when the service ended because I did not want to leave. I never wanted to leave. I never wanted that feeling of closeness to God to end. I knew that bringing me to this church was another giant step toward me getting that emotional connection to God that I was so desperately seeking. All I needed now was my understanding of God the Father and the Old Testament opened up to me. I knew that once I had that understanding of God, my connection would be complete. I was almost there. After over twenty years of seeking an emotional connection and understanding of God, I was almost there to it. Every experience in my life was teaching me something new about God.

I learned many lessons from that church service that day, and the most important one is that a real church does not consist of a specific building or a certain set of circumstances. People can worship God anytime, anywhere, and God can be among them in any situation. Anytime two or more believers gather anywhere with a heart yearning for God, a church is created. The church is a matter of the heart, not of bricks and concrete. I also learned a good lesson about not judging people and situations so hastily. These casually dressed people sitting on battered folding chairs in a high school gymnasium were some of the friendliest and spirit-filled people that I ever had the pleasure of meeting. I had finally found the church that I belonged in, and I knew I was there to stay.

~

Mouse decided that since she could not attend Bible school like she had when I was a child, she wanted us to do a Bible study together. I had participated in Bible studies at several churches on various biblical topics, but those Bible studies were on random topics that I could not quite fit together in my mind. While those studies had given me different glimpses of God and Jesus, they were like scattered puzzle pieces with no picture to work from to connect them. Each Bible study had given me a small piece of an unknown foundation that I was struggling to uncover.

The Bible study we chose to do centered on the various ways that God had spoken to people throughout biblical times and was intended to help students distinguish between the actual voice of God and those of false prophets and teachers. As I flipped through the workbook, I was surprised to find that it began with the story of creation and worked mostly in chronological order to the last book of the Old Testament. I was pleased to find a study that would bring me through the Old Testament in the order in which it had happened. I was hopeful that it would show me the completed picture of God's work in the world.

After a brief discussion, it was decided that we would take turns reading the lessons aloud and that I would do most of the work in finding the answers to the study questions. Little One was the most like a teacher among us, and she delighted in being the first one to start the lessons. She slowly read the story of creation from the first chapter of Genesis and then paused for reflection when she was finished.

"God has awesome power," Mouse breathed. "He spoke heaven and earth into existence."

"What was God doing before He created the world?" Bug asked. She had temporarily let go of her worrying to join us for the Bible lessons.

Little One glanced at what she had just read. "The Bible says God was hovering over the waters," she replied.

"I find it difficult to understand that God has always existed," Little Lisa said. "It's hard for me to believe that something could have no beginning and no end."

"Nobody created God," Little One said. "He always was. He existed even before He created time and space."

We all stopped talking for a moment to ponder God's amazing existence. Bug broke into our thoughts by asking, "Did God ever get bored before He created the world? It must have been boring to Him just to hover around and do nothing."

"I don't think God has ever felt bored," Little One replied. "God delights in Himself. I think Jesus was always with Him. He probably created the world simply because it pleased Him to do so."

"Continue with the reading," I told Little One impatiently. "Let's get on to the story of Adam and Eve,"

Little One returned to reading, and we listened as she recounted the story of how Satan had deceived Adam and Eve into disobeying God. The passage ended with God having banished Adam and Eve from the Garden of Eden.

"Stop right there," I said. "That is where my mind first breaks about God. He is supposed to be a loving God, yet in the first book of the Bible, He is already handing out major punishment. He kicked His children out of their home and into a world to fend for themselves under all kinds of curses. How can God expect us to believe that He is loving and merciful when one of the first things He does in the Bible is hand out such a punishment to the people He created?"

Mouse put down the cookie that she was eating and brushed her hands on our pants. "Your mind is so negatively slanted," she said. "Of course, you would view that part of the creation story in such a pessimistic way."

"If you can tell me one positive thing about that story then tomorrow you can have all of the treats that your heart desires," I challenged.

A small smile played on Mouse's lips. "You don't have enough money to buy all of the treats I want," she said.

"I am not worried about it," I said confidently. "Even you cannot deny that God threw the children that He supposedly loved out of the garden for their first mistake."

"Do you think Adam and Eve should not have been dealt any consequences for disobeying God?" Mouse asked.

"Sure, they should have received a consequence for their action," I said. "But was cursing them and throwing them out of His presence an appropriate punishment for the sin that they committed? They simply ate some fruit that God told them not to eat. That was hardly a major crime."

Mouse was slow and deliberate in her response. "God told them not to eat that fruit because He knew how much it would hurt them," she said. "God told them they would die if they ate that fruit. He cared about what would happen to them if they ate it."

I shifted uncomfortably in my chair. "If they were going to die from eating that fruit, then that should have been punishment enough," I said. "He didn't have to add to that punishment by cursing them and throwing them out of the garden."

"God threw them out of the garden because of His great love and mercy for them," Mouse said.

"His great love and mercy?" I laughed. "What would He have done to them if He hated them?"

"God did not throw Adam and Eve out of the garden with the same mindset that your mother threw you out of the house when you were a child," Mouse said quietly.

Mouse's words caught me off guard, and I did not know how to respond.

"You are confusing those incidents," Mouse continued. "If this is where your mind first broke about God, then this is where it needs fixing."

My eyes welled with tears as I remembered the terror and loneliness I had felt whenever my mother had locked me out of the house as a child, sometimes for days at a time. I imagined that was how Adam and Eve also felt when God banished them from the garden.

"The main reason that God banished Adam and Eve from the garden was that the tree of life was also in that garden," Mouse went on. "God loved them too much to allow them to eat from the tree of life. He did not want them to live forever."

I wiped a fallen tear from my cheek. "That makes no sense that God wanted Adam and Eve to die," I said.

"God did not want them to die in the same way your mother kept telling you she wished you were dead," Mouse said. "God wanted them to die so that they could live with Him forever."

"You are not making any sense!" I said angrily. "You are only confusing me more."

Mouse lifted her eyes upward and said, "God, please help me explain this to Lisa in a way that will help her to understand you." After a moment of silence, she took a deep breath and said, "When Adam and Eve disobeyed God, they committed the first human sin. They ate fruit from a tree that enabled them to know both good and evil. They were then in a sinful state. All sin separates people from a holy God, so when they disobeyed God, they became spiritually separated from Him. They were then in a spiritually fallen state. Do you understand this so far?"

I sniffed and rubbed more tears from my eyes. "Yes," I said.

Mouse soldiered on with her words carefully, waiting for guidance from her strong connection to God. "God was very sad about Adam and Eve's fallen state," she continued. "He knew that if they also ate from the tree of life, they would remain alive in their sinful and spiritually separated state from Him forever. He wanted to restore them. Therefore, He had to banish them from the garden away from that tree of life. If He sent them away, He could start His plan of salvation for them in motion. By letting them die physically, He could eventually give them eternal life through the saving work of His son Jesus. He would make that way of salvation to forgive them for their sin and restore their spiritual state. If they ate from that tree of life and lived forever in their fallen state, He would not have been able to save and restore them spiritually. That banishment from the garden was more about God's love and mercy for them than about His punishment for their sin."

My heart quickened, and my eyes dried up quickly as I began to digest Mouse's words. A light as bright as the sun started to implode in my mind. I was stunned by this new revelation. How could it be that I had never known the creation story from this loving viewpoint?

Mouse felt the growing light of wisdom expanding from my head into my heart, and she became excited. "Can you now understand what I know?" she asked.

I caught Mouse's feeling of joy. "Yes!" I exclaimed. "I can understand God's love for them now."

Mouse clapped her hands together. "You mean God's love for *us,* " she corrected. "He did not make the plan of salvation just for Adam and Eve. He made that plan of salvation for every human that has ever lived—to reconcile us back to Him and allow us to spend eternity with Him."

"But why should every person need salvation because of what Adam and Eve did?" I asked.

"Every person is born in a fallen and sinful state," Mouse replied. "Every person needs salvation to be restored spiritually in God's sight."

"The reason for and meaning of salvation is clear to me now," I said. "Now how can I take that love that I can see God had for Adam and Eve and apply it to myself? How can I believe that God really loves *me?* I feel so worthless and undeserving of His love."

"I think your emotional issues about God are beyond any of us being able to help you with them," Little One said. "Perhaps it would be best for you to take Pastor Dave's suggestion and seek out a Christian therapist."

"I have my therapist," I protested.

"I am not telling you to give up your therapist," Little One said. "I am only saying that maybe a few sessions with a Christian therapist would help you to be able to separate God's feelings for you from your mother's feelings and actions toward you."

I mulled over the idea. "I will give it some serious thought," I said.

"Your mother ruined your childhood and your sense of self-worth," Little One said. "Don't allow her to ruin the most important relationship you could ever have."

~

The next day, I began to mull over the idea of talking to a Christian therapist. The website for my church indicated that there was a counselor on the staff. I decided to speak with Pastor Dennis to get more information.

I found Pastor Dennis seated in his office preparing his sermon notes for Sunday morning service. He greeted me warmly and gestured for me to have a seat. "What brings you here today?" he asked.

"I would like some information about the counselor who is on the staff at the church," I said.

Pastor Dennis nodded and pushed aside his paperwork to give me his full attention. "We have a psychologist who has a practice at the church. Dr. Flannery has thirty years of experience in Christian therapy. She has an excellent reputation among our church members and in the community."

"I already have a therapist, and I am not looking to replace her," I said hastily. "She is a good therapist who has been devoted to helping me improve the quality of my life for many years. But she does not do Christian-based therapy, and I am having trouble understanding who God is and accepting that He loves me."

Pastor Dennis reached into his desk and then handed me a business card. "This is Dr. Flannery's office number," he said. "Give her a call and see if she can help you."

I glanced at the card before shoving it into my pocket. "Thank you," I said as I stood up to leave. "I am sorry for having disturbed you."

"You did not disturb me," Pastor Dennis said. "If you have a few minutes, why don't you sit back down and talk to me for a moment."

I sat back down and gave him a curious look.

"What exactly do you find difficult to understand about God?" Pastor Dennis asked.

"I have always thought that God is mean and demanding," I explained. "I did not get a good view of Him after I tried to read the Old Testament. Just recently, somebody helped me see that I have the wrong concept of Him. I understand now that God is good and merciful, but I only have that concept of Him in my head, not in my heart. I find it difficult to believe that He could love a person as damaged as myself."

Pastor Dennis reached for his Bible. "Let me tell you a little bit about God's character," he said. "I am going to get this information straight from His word." He opened his Bible and began to flip through the pages. "God had a tremendous love for us at the beginning of time," he said. "He still has that same love for us today. It will never change."

"The world seems to have gotten so far away from God," I frowned. "People are pushing Him out of everything today, especially out of their lives."

"People may be changing about God, but God will never change about people," Pastor Dennis said. "No matter how much they try to ignore Him or push Him away, He is still here loving people and hoping that they will turn to Him. God's character will never change. His character was the same when He created the world as it is now."

"I know God is supposed to be good," I said.

"God is more than good," Pastor Dennis chuckled. He put down his Bible, reached into his desk, and pulled out a worn notebook. "I've written down some of God's character traits according to the bible," he said. "Maybe it would help you to understand the Old Testament better if you understood God's character better."

"Please," I said.

"Certainly," Pastor Dennis said as he opened the notebook and reached across the desk for his reading glasses. "These are some notes that I jotted down about God's character to help me prepare my sermons," he said. "Ephesians 2:4 tells us that God loves. John 14:6 says that He is truthful. 1 John 1:5 says that He is holy. Acts 17:31 says that He is just."

"Nothing in there about being mean," I said.

"Some people think that because God is just it means that He is mean," Pastor Dennis said. "God does judge sin, but He also shows compassion and grace. Psalm 130:4 says that He offers forgiveness. You will note that the Psalms are part of the Old Testament. If you want a good idea of who God is, I suggest that you read Psalm 103. It is one of my favorites. It will give you a great picture of God's true character."

I made a mental note of that.

Pastor Dennis looked down at his notebook again. "1 Timothy 1:17 tells us that God is infinite," he continued. "Psalm 139 7-12 lets us know that God exists everywhere. Isaiah 40:28 tells us that He knows everything, and Revelation 19:6 says that He has all power and authority." He closed his notebook and placed in on his desk. "Does that help you any?" he asked.

"Yes," I said. "Now if I could only process that information in my heart and not just in my head. Thank you for giving me that information."

"See if Dr. Flannery can help you," Pastor Dennis encouraged.

Not sure what to do, I returned home and prayed about seeing Dr. Flannery. Since the suggestion had come from Pastor Dennis, I wondered if it was a suggestion from God to me. I knew that if the idea was coming from God that I could trust something good would come from it, so I finally picked up the phone and dialed the number on the card that Pastor Dennis had given me. Dr. Flannery's secretary answered, and I explained who I was and that I was seeking some Christian counseling.

"Have you ever been here before?" the secretary asked.

"No," I replied.

"Dr. Flannery does not accept any insurance at this time," the secretary said. "She asks that all clients pay cash. Will that be a problem for you?"

I swallowed hard. I had not thought about having to pay Dr. Flannery for her services. I had assumed that Christian counselors worked free, but it occurred to me then that Dr. Flannery had bills to pay like the rest of us do. I was still on a fixed income and paying cash out of my pocket would be nearly impossible for me. "How much does she charge?" I asked.

"Fifty dollars an hour," the secretary said.

I felt my face grow red with shame, knowing I could not afford even that much. "I will have to call you back," I said hastily.

Why would God lead me to a Christian therapist that He knew I could not afford? He knew that I was on a fixed income. I checked my bank account against my bills and found that I could pay for two sessions, but no more than that. "God, why would you send me to a therapist when you know I can only afford to go twice?" I asked. "You know the mental disorders that I have. I will need more than two sessions. I have already been seeing mental health professionals for over twenty years! What good will two sessions do for somebody with all of my issues?"

I thought I heard God's small, quiet voice reply to me, "Just go to the two sessions and let Me worry about the rest."

"Lord, are you talking to me or am I just talking to myself? I have such a difficult time knowing if you are talking to me or not."

With a slight level of uncertainty, I picked up the phone and called Dr. Flannery's secretary again. I made an appointment, but I did not mention the fact that I could only afford two sessions. If God wanted me to talk to Dr. Flannery, He would have to work out the financial details for me. "God, please don't let me be embarrassed by having me look like a poor pauper," I begged Him after I had made the appointment. "I do not want to be a charity case."

I was not sure whether I was following God's will or not, but I decided to trust my instincts that I was and see where God was leading me this time.

# Seventeen

*Bearing with one another, and forgiving one*
*another, if anyone has a complaint against another;*
*even as Christ forgave you, so you also must do.*
*(Colossians 3:13)*

Dr. Flannery was a small, middle-aged woman with gray hair pulled into a tight bun on the top of her head. She was wearing a red-and-green plaid dress that made me think of Christmas even though it was the middle of summer. She shook my hand and greeted me warmly as she ushered me into her office. The office was drab, with worn brown furniture and matching carpet. I sat in one of the two oversized recliners and looked at the large white cross hanging on the wall above her desk. "It's nice to meet you, Lisa," she said cheerfully as she pulled her desk chair close to me. She sat down and leaned toward me.

"I feel a little uncomfortable right now," I said.

Dr. Flannery cocked her head. "Do you have any idea what is making you feel uncomfortable?" she asked.

"I already have a therapist," I admitted. "I have been seeing her for several years."

Dr. Flannery leaned back in her chair. "I see," she said. "If you already have a therapist, what made you come to see me today?"

My eyes traveled back to the cross on the wall. "My therapist does not do Christian-based therapy," I replied. "I don't think she can help me with some issues that I am having with God. I hope that you can help me with some of those issues."

"I do not usually treat people who are already seeing another therapist," Dr. Flannery said. "It could become a problem when somebody is seeing multiple therapists. Each therapist has their approach to treatment, and there could be a conflict of interest."

"Okay," I sighed. "I am sorry that I wasted your time." I stood up to leave.

"Wait a minute." Dr. Flannery nodded toward the recliner, indicating that I should return to my seat. "I am curious to know more about you and your situation. Several years is a long time to continue to see a therapist. Do you have a certain situation in your life that is taking that long to resolve?"

I sat back down and shook my head. "It's not one particular situation," I told her. "I have a mental illness."

"What have you been diagnosed with?" Dr. Flannery asked.

"A few of them," I replied. "Bipolar Disorder, Borderline Personality Disorder, and Multiple Personality Disorder."

Dr. Flannery hesitated. "Multiple Personality Disorder is known as Dissociative Identity Disorder now," she informed me. "Are you sure that is the disorder you have?"

"Yes," I said.

"Dissociative Identity Disorder is a rare disorder that I do not have any experience treating," Dr. Flannery said.

"I am not here for treatment for any of my mental illnesses," I said. "My regular therapist is treating me for those. I am only looking for some Christian counseling from you."

"They may not be separate issues," Dr. Flannery said. "Having mental illness can affect the way that you think and feel. That may have a direct impact on your relationship with God. Why don't you tell me about the issues that you say you are having with God?"

I began to explain my tendency to see God and Jesus as distinctly separate beings. "I do not understand the Old Testament too well," I told her. "From what I have read, my concept of God the Father is that He can be mean and harsh. He handed out many rules and laws that He must have known would be impossible to follow. I sometimes feel like He was purposely setting us up to fail." I paused. "I feel guilty for seeing God that way," I continued. "In the New Testament, I can see how loving He is. He sent His only son to die for our sins."

"Lisa, you are not the only person to have a distorted image of God," Dr. Flanner said.

I was surprised. "Other people are as confused about God as I am?" I asked.

"Certainly," Dr. Flannery said. "I deal with people all the time who have distortions about who God is. You are not alone with that."

I thought about what my personalities had told me about my relationship with God versus my relationship with my mother. "Somebody once told me that my relationship with my mother had affected my view of God," I said.

"That is interesting," Dr. Flannery said. "Tell me about your family and your background. Perhaps we can make sense of the correlation between God and your mother."

I spent the next half hour telling Dr. Flannery about my childhood and my abusive past with my mother as well as the sexual abuse that I went through with my Grandfather. My background was so scarred with trauma that half an hour was not nearly enough time to relate my entire story to her, so I condensed it and told her what I felt were the most traumatic offenses.

"You certainly have been through some difficult circumstances," Dr. Flannery acknowledged.

"I am trying to let God heal my mind and my heart," I said.

"For you to heal you need to have the correct image of God," Dr. Flannery said.

I was relieved that she understood my situation. "That is why I came to you," I said. "I am hoping that you can help me put that distorted picture of God together for me. I think I am making progress with it, but I seem to need a little extra help. When Pastor Dennis mentioned to me that the church has a Christian psychologist on board, I felt as if God were leading me here." I went on to tell her about my alters helping me to see God's loving mercy in sending Adam and Eve out of the Garden of Eden.

"Do you understand what the Old Testament is about?" Dr. Flannery asked.

"Not so much," I admitted. "It has been difficult for me to read it. It seems so…dry."

"It might not seem too dry if you understood the background and what is going on in it," Dr. Flannery stated.

"Help me to understand it," I begged.

"The Old Testament is a love story between God and His chosen people," Dr. Flannery explained. "It's also a wonderful piece of history."

"I do know that God chose the people of Israel to be His chosen people," I said.

"God chose Israel as the nation that He wanted to speak through," Dr. Flannery said. "Through His interactions with Israel, He wanted to show other nations that He alone is God."

"But why did He give His people so many rules and laws that would be so impossible for them to follow?" I asked. "In the first few books of the Bible, it seems that all I read are the rules that God handed them."

"God did not set up people to fail when he gave the Israelites those laws," Dr. Flannery said. "The first thing that you should understand about God is how holy He is. Because of His holiness, He cannot stand even the slightest sin in any form. It is not that He is trying to be mean; that is how holy He is. His laws were not made because He is impossible to please; they had to do with that holiness. Being holy is a part of God's character. Also, those rules were there because He loved the Israelites so much that He wanted the best lives for them."

"He had to have known that the Israelites would fail at keeping all of those laws," I said.

"Of course, He knew that they would fail," Dr. Flannery agreed. "The Israelites were imperfect human beings just like we all are. God knew they would fail, which is why He set up the system of offerings so that He could forgive them for failing. God set up those laws so that people would see their need for a savior, not for them to feel like failures. However, God requires a blood sacrifice for sins. That is why in the Old Testament, the Israelites performed animal sacrifices to atone for their sins. At that time in history, the Israelites did not have Jesus' blood as a sacrifice for their sins. The death of God's son became the one perfect blood sacrifice that forever abolished the animal sacrifice system."

"I have heard that before," I said. "But why was God angry with the Israelites so much of the time? You said the Old Testament is a love story, but God seems to be angry with the people in it."

"God was only angry with them because they would continually fall away from Him and worship false gods," Dr. Flannery said. "God repeatedly proved to them that He was their God and that He wanted to love them and take care of them, but invariably the Israelites would go astray from Him and start worshipping other foreign gods. In its simplest form, the Old Testament is the story of God's love and devotion to His people, and how He kept pursuing them and how He kept trying to get them to return to Him after they would turn away from Him."

I had never heard about the Old Testament in that context before, and Dr. Flannery's simple explanation was a new and exciting revelation to me. With that fresh understanding, I was eager to try rereading the Old Testament with a completely different perspective of God.

"I haven't even been here for an hour, and you have already helped me so much," I said. "In all my years of being a Christian, I never knew that the Old Testament was primarily a love story about God pursuing His people because they kept turning away from Him."

"Now you've got it!" Dr. Flannery exclaimed. She seemed excited that I had understood her explanation so quickly.

"I am confused about something though," I said. "If the Jews are God's chosen people, then how do the non-Jews like us know that we are also God's people? What if Jesus died only for the Jewish people?"

"That is a good question," Dr. Flannery smiled. "Did you know that many Jewish people in the New Testament rejected Jesus as their savior? Some of the Jews to this day do not believe that Jesus is the savior."

I was incredulous. "How could God's own chosen people not believe that His son is the savior?" I asked.

"In the New Testament, the Jewish people were not expecting a savior like Jesus," Dr. Flannery explained. "They were expecting a savior who would be a mighty warrior and fight to restore Israel. Some of the Jews today are still waiting for that mighty warrior to come. This ties in with your question about how we can know that we as Gentiles are also God's people. Because so many Jewish people rejected Jesus, God made salvation available to everybody who would believe in Jesus—Jews and Gentiles alike. You can read about the inclusion of the Gentiles in the book of Acts."

I could hardly believe that there was still so much about the Bible that I did not know and still so much for me to learn. I still did not know some of the basic concepts. "I am now positive that God led me to you," I said. "You have been more helpful to me than some of the Bible studies that I have attended."

"I am glad that I could help you today. My sessions rarely go this well on the first day," Dr. Flannery said. "I am concerned about your relationship with your mother possibly affecting your view of God. Perhaps we should explore that further. It is obvious to me by the things that you have told me that you have very low self-esteem and a poor sense of identity. I do not think that is only because of the way that your mother treated you. I also think the sexual abuse that you experienced is a large part of the reason why you see yourself so negatively. It also appears that you have some serious trust issues that are affecting your relationship with God. If you would like to come back and have another session with me next week, maybe I can help you make sense of all of it."

I thought about my financial situation and felt my face blush. "I would like that," I said. "But I thought you would not want to see me again because I am seeing the other therapist."

Dr. Flannery hesitated. "It's not the ideal situation," She said. "It would be better for you to choose one therapist for treatment. In this case, since I do not have experience with some of your mental illnesses, I will go ahead and counsel you for the short term while you are seeing another therapist. However, I would highly suggest that you also let your other therapist know that you are seeing me. When it comes to your treatment, it is best to be up front with everybody and try to have us all on the same page."

"I will tell her," I promised. I stood up and stuck out my hand toward her. "I cannot thank you enough for agreeing to talk to me today."

"You are welcome," Dr. Flannery said. "Before you go let me give you a list of Bible studies that I think may help you."

I was excited to get home and start reading the Old Testament with my new understanding of it. As I was leaving, I ran into Pastor Dennis in the parking lot. "I just came out of my first session with Dr. Flannery," I told him.

"Good for you!" Pastor Dennis said. "By the look on your face, I trust it went well."

"It went more than well," I told him. "It went great. She helped me to see that the Old Testament is a story about God loving and pursuing His people."

"That's right," Pastor Dennis nodded. "I hope that will make it easier for you to understand it as you read it."

"I am sure that it will." I started toward my car and then turned to face him again. "Pastor Dennis, did you know that many Jews today reject Jesus as being the Savior?"

"It's not just the Jews," Pastor Dennis frowned. "Many people in the world today reject Jesus as their Savior."

"I am going to pray for the whole world," I said. "And one day I am going to write a book that I hope will reach lots of people to help them know that God is still pursuing people today."

Pastor Dennis put his hand gently on my shoulder and smiled at me. "Many people have difficult lives," he said. "Perhaps God will use your difficulties to help shine some of His light into their darkness."

"Praise God," I said, and then I headed home to delve into the Old Testament.

~

"I am so excited because the Old Testament is no longer dry reading to me," I told Dr. Flannery during my second session with her the following week.

"That's great," Dr. Flannery said. "Are you reading it in order chapter by chapter or are you skipping around in it?"

"I am reading it in order now," I said. "I find it much easier to understand reading it in order. I think one of the reasons I was having so much trouble understanding it is because I used to skip around and read only the parts that held my interest. It is all interesting to me now." I paused. "Although I do still tend to skip over the begat sections," I admitted. "Such as where it says this person begat that person and so on."

"What book are you currently reading?" Dr. Flannery asked.

"Deuteronomy," I replied. "I am getting into where God gives the rules and regulations to the Israelites. Did you know that Moses wrote the first five books of the Bible?"

"Of course," Dr. Flannery laughed. "Those first five books are known as the Torah. Did you look into any of those Bible studies that I listed for you?"

"I went to the library and found one of them there," I said. "I also found many other reference books there to help me understand the Bible."

Dr. Flannery looked surprised. "You didn't know some books were written to help people understand the Bible?" she asked.

I shook my head. "I didn't know that," I said. "I never looked for those types of books before. Some of them are very interesting. I'm reading one of them that is helping me understand the Old Testament called *The Bible for Blockheads* by Douglas Connelly."

"If you want to read an awesome book about God's character and attributes, I highly suggest reading *Our God Is Awesome* by Tony Evans," Dr. Flannery suggested. "That is one of the best books I have ever read about God."

"I will be sure to check that one out," I said.

"You certainly sound more excited about reading the Bible than you did last week," Dr. Flannery remarked.

"That's because it's the word of the holy and majestic Lord," I said. "I have always felt awe when reading the Bible, but it has become much more precious to me now that I know it is a love story between God and all of His people, including us Gentiles. How powerful and wonderful He is!"

"Let's not forget how loving and merciful He also is," Dr. Flannery said. "Those are important attributes of God for you to focus on, considering your poor sense of self-concept."

I was quiet for a moment while I considered that. Dr. Flannery patiently waited for me to get my thoughts together. "For most of my life my mother abused me physically and emotionally," I said slowly. "She told me that I was worthless and ugly so many times that that is how I see myself now."

"It must have been challenging for you to hear those words from the person who is supposed to love you unconditionally," Dr. Flannery said. "But just because your mother spoke those kinds of words to you does not make them true, and it does not have to define who you are."

"It's hard not to believe those words after having them beaten into your head for so many years," I said.

"I understand that, but it is possible to change your way of thinking about yourself," Dr. Flannery said. "It may not be easy, but it is possible. You can start that change by correctly seeing God and then understanding how much He loves and values you. To change how you think about yourself you must first change how you think about God, and it's obvious that you have already made progress with that over the years."

"God has been helping me to see Him differently in many ways for many years," I said. "I realize now that sometimes God will correct me or let me face the negative consequences of my actions, but that doesn't mean that He is out to get me or that He doesn't love me anymore."

"If you can believe that it is truly a major step for you," Dr. Flannery said. "You have done half my work for me already. Lisa, I think that you are at a point in your life now where you can understand that people like your mother and your grandfather are sick people themselves. They have their own set of mental health issues. Unfortunately, they negatively affected you and your emotional health with their issues. The best that you can do now is let God deal with those people who hurt you and let Him heal you from the damage that they caused you. You do not have to be a victim of their mental health issues any longer. You are an adult now, and you can choose not to be the victim that you were forced to be when you were a child. I can see that you are choosing to let go of being that victim now."

"I am still sad," I said. "I find it devastating that I lost so much of my life already. My entire childhood was taken from me, and I can't get any of those lost years back."

"You cannot get them back, and it is okay to mourn for those lost years," Dr. Flannery said. "But you are still alive, and every day that you wake up breathing is another day to find happiness. God can help you find that happiness."

"I am trying to forgive the people who hurt me," I said. "It is so difficult to do."

"Forgiving them does not mean that you have to agree with the things that they did to you or that they said to you," Dr. Flannery said. "Nor does it mean that you have to accept or share their views of who you are."

"Forgiveness for me means letting go of any hatred or bitterness that I feel towards them," I said.

"It also means healing the emotional damage that they caused you," Dr. Flannery said. "Do you think God views you as ugly or worthless?"

I thought about that. "I guess He did not send His son to die for somebody that He thinks is worthless," I said.

"That is exactly right," Dr. Flannery said.

"I know that, but I have a hard time believing it," I sighed. "I've done some pretty rotten things in my life. Sometimes I think that God won't forgive me for the worst things I have done."

"Is that reality?" Dr. Flannery asked. "Is there anything so terrible that God can't forgive? When you feel you aren't forgiven, you are saying that the death of Jesus wasn't an adequate penalty for your sin."

"I would never think that," I said.

"It says in 1 John 1:9 that if we confess our sins, He is faithful and just to forgive us our sins and to cleanse us from all unrighteousness," Dr. Flannery pointed out. "Are you calling God a liar?"

"I know God does not lie," I said. "It's just that I still struggle with guilt sometimes."

"Does guilt and condemnation come from God?" Dr. Flannery asked. "Or does it come straight from the devil?" She reached for the bible that was sitting on her desk and flipped through the pages. "Acts 5:19 says: *'Repent therefore and be converted, that your sins may be blotted out, so that times of refreshing may come from the presence of the Lord.'* As for your guilt, Romans 8:1 says: *'There is therefore now no condemnation to those who are in Christ Jesus, who do not walk according to the flesh, but according to the spirit.'"*

I clasped my hands together and thought about the goodness of God.

"Here is one more scripture," Dr. Flannery said. "Listen carefully to this word from God. He is speaking to you and to all of the other people like you who also have a difficult time feeling forgiven and who struggle with guilt. *For God did not send His Son into the world to condemn the*

*world, but that the world through Him might be saved. He who believes in*
*Him is not condemned, but he who does not believe is condemned already*
*because he has not believed in the name of the only begotten Son of God.'*
That is John 3:17-18. Do you truly believe that Jesus is your savior?"

I closed my eyes and felt one lone tear trickle down my cheek. I felt
overwhelmed by the love of God for a messed-up sinner like me. "I
believe," I whispered.

Dr. Flannery closed her bible and placed it back on her desk. "Then
you are saved," she said. "You are truly in the right place with God, and it
is okay to stop feeling guilty and to feel joy. Lisa, it is okay to feel good. It
is okay to feel happy. It is even okay to like yourself. God loves you, and
God has saved you. Give all of your hurt and your despair about your past
to God and let him heal your heart. He will not just slap a Band-Aid on
your wounds, so you can't see them. He will heal them, so they don't hurt
anymore."

I felt another tear run down my cheek as I lifted my head and gave her
a small smile. "What about all of the mental illnesses that I was diagnosed
with?" I asked.

"What about them?" Dr. Flannery asked in return.

"Does having mental illnesses make me a flawed person?"

"Do you feel like less of a person because you have mental illnesses?"

"Yes," I said. "My symptoms have left me unable to work a full-time
job at this point, and everyday functioning is often difficult for me. I
struggle with feeling sick and tired from my medication side effects. I have
frequent mood swings and alter personalities. And I haven't been able to
have too many close relationships because my symptoms quickly wear
other people out."

"I acknowledge that you have great difficulties in your current life,"
Dr. Flannery said. "Some of that may be related to chemical issues in your
brain, and some of it may be damage caused by environmental factors.
Even though you have so many difficulties, they do not have to define you
in the same way that the abuse from your past does not have to define you.

God has defined you. He defined you the minute Jesus died on that cross. Why don't you try asking God how you can use all of the difficulties with which you struggle? He may not heal you from all of your symptoms, but He can use it for good if you ask Him to and then allow Him to."

Dr. Flannery had just verified what I had already been thinking for some time. Perhaps this was God's way of proving to me that my thinking was on the right track. God has presented me with several opportunities to witness, but I am awkward around most people. What I want to do is to write a book to witness to other people who go through what I have gone through. Do you think God would allow me to witness that way?"

"I have no idea what His plans are for you in the future. You would have to ask Him that," Dr. Flannery chuckled. "If God allowed you to witness through writing, what kinds of things would you like to say to other people who are also struggling with their lives?"

I leaned my head against the back of the recliner. "I would tell them that suicide is not the answer," I said. "Substance abuse is not the answer. Self-mutilation is not the answer. I want them to know that there is only one answer to their trouble and their pain. That answer is Jesus."

Dr. Flannery looked at me silently for a moment, her curious eyes searching my determined ones. Suddenly her face broke into a bright smile. "Lisa, this is only your second session with me," she said. "But I don't think you need to see me anymore. You say that you have been seeking to understand God the Father for many years, but I think that you found Him along the way, and you did not even realize it. You said that He has revealed Himself to you in many ways through different people. Now it's our turn to be one of those people that He uses to reveal Himself to other people." She paused and looked thoughtful. "I think the next step in your journey is to make peace with your mother," she added. "Your relationship with her might be somewhat better now that you're an adult, but I see that you still have a lot of hurt in your heart. Give all of that hurt to God so that you can let it go and be effective in your witnessing."

"I think I already have," I said.

Dr. Flannery shook her head. "I am pretty sure that you haven't," she said.

I knew that I would never see Dr. Flannery again as a patient. The two sessions that I had with her left a major impact on me, not only about understanding the Old Testament but also understanding how I needed to continue to improve myself and my walk with God. I stopped seeing her and resumed my sessions with my regular therapist, but my decision to see a Christian therapist even for the two sessions that God had given me turned out to be one of the best decisions of my life.

# Eighteen

*For my life is spent with grief, and my years with sighing; my strength fails because of my iniquity, and my bones waste away. (Psalm 31:10)*

After my two sessions with Dr. Flannery, dealing with my mother became a little less tense, but my interactions with Little Lisa remained stressful. I continued to see her as the bad part of myself, the part of me that neither my mother nor God could love.

Little Lisa resented my attitude toward her, and she did very little to cooperate when it came to making sure my daily functioning was going smoothly. Our constant arguing caused chronic stress for Little One, who tried to be the mediator between us. Often Little One would try to get Little Lisa and me to see each other's good points, but Little Lisa and I were both convinced that neither of us had any redeeming qualities.

"You created Little Lisa," Little One would insist. "We are your disorder. How can you hate something that you created?"

"That is the same way that Lisa feels about God," Mouse said. "She feels that God hates who He created."

"My goodness, Lisa," Little One sighed. "Your relationships with God, your mother, and Little Lisa are so tied together in such a psychological way that I don't know if they can ever be straightened out."

"If straightening them out means forgiving my mother or liking Little Lisa then I seriously doubt it," I said.

"I have an idea. Let's go back in time," Little One said. "Let's go deep into your memory and see what was happening to you when you first created Little Lisa."

"Forget it," I said. "No matter how much you try to analyze me, you are not a therapist."

"If we can find the root of the problem between you and Little Lisa maybe we can fix it," Little One suggested.

"I am not interested in fixing my relationship with her," I said stubbornly.

"I am not interested in it either," Little Lisa said in a tone that matched my own.

Little One was not one to give up easily. She was convinced that if I looked back far enough into my memory, I would find out why my relationship with Little Lisa had developed in such a negative way. Although Little Lisa and I continued to insist that we were not interested in the idea, Little One's effort at reconciliation eventually began to wear on me. Little One had the power to be quite persuasive.

"Shouldn't something like that be done in the safety of our therapist's office?" Bug fretted.

"Lisa seems emotionally stronger lately, and we have God to help us," Little One assured Bug.

Bug began to wring her hands nervously. "I don't know about this," she said. "I sense trouble ahead."

"Do you ever stop worrying about everything, Bug?" Little One snapped. "Not everything has to be met with such dread and anxiety."

"This will if you keep pursuing it," Bug said.

"Shush, Bug," Little One said. "I am only trying to help Lisa."

"May God help us," Bug said.

"Of course, He will," Little One said. She then turned her attention back to me. "Are you willing to try it?" she asked.

"If you are not going to leave me alone about it," I sighed.

"I strongly feel like it is something that should be done," Little One said. "I trust my feeling about it."

"Maybe you should try to hypnotize Lisa," Mouse said.

Little One shook her head. "I do not have a clue how to hypnotize a person," she said. "Besides, hypnosis reminds me of the occult and witchcraft. God warns us in the Bible not to get involved in those types of things." She paused and then instructed me to sit down and relax. "Can you think back to what was happening when you created any of us?" she asked.

I struggled to find any piece of information regarding the creation of my alters in my memory. "No," I said. "It seems like you all just popped out of nowhere in my head."

"Think hard about Little Lisa," Little One encouraged. "Tell me what was happening when she first appeared."

I saw nothing but vast darkness in my mind, and I quickly became frustrated. "My mind is empty," I said. "I don't see anything."

Unwilling to give up, Little One was silent for a moment as she thought about it. "Wait a minute," she said. "I will bet that you have pushed that memory away from your mind and Little Lisa is holding that memory of her creation for you. It must have been too difficult for you to bear, so you gave it to Little Lisa to protect yourself from it." She turned to Little Lisa. "Am I correct about this?" she asked her. "Do you hold the memory of your creation for Lisa?"

"Leave me alone," Little Lisa snapped.

"Tell us what happened," Little One said.

"Damn you, Little One," Little Lisa growled. "Leave well enough alone."

"Lisa needs to know what happened," Little One said quietly. "Don't you want to know what happened, Lisa?"

A feeling of dread swept over me, and I swallowed the huge lump that was in my throat. I had a sense that this was going too far, and the need to protect myself was overwhelming. I wanted to run, but I felt rooted to my spot, like a curious spectator watching a horrible accident about to happen. I was too compelled to look away. "Tell me," I told Little Lisa.

Little Lisa hesitated for a long moment, unsure whether she should move ahead. Sensing my desire to remember, she slowly began her story. "You were five years old," she said. "It was winter. I do not remember what month it was, but it was freezing outside, and there was snow on the ground. It was nighttime, and you were in bed, unable to sleep because you were frightened. Your mother was awake and on another drunken rampage. She had been arguing violently with your father for several hours, and he finally left the house, but your mother's rampage didn't end after his departure." She paused. "Should I keep going?" she asked.

"It sounds as if it were just a typical night," I said. "Keep going."

"Your mother still had wrath to expend," Little Lisa continued. "She came to your bedroom and threw open your door. She began shouting at you for having been born and ruining her life."

"That still sounds typical," I said. "I should have been well used to hearing that."

"Yes," Little Lisa said. "However, that night, she dragged you out of bed and down the stairs and then threw you out of the house. You were outside in the cold and snow in your pajamas, with no coat and nothing on your feet. You tried to get back into the house, but the door was locked."

As Little Lisa spoke, a faint picture began to form in my mind. I could see myself standing on the porch, shivering violently from the cold. My feet felt numb from standing in the snow. I could see myself knocking on the door and crying hysterically. A feeling of desperation began to wash over me. If my mother did not let me back into the house, I was going to freeze to death.

"Suddenly you saw a light go off in the house," Little Lisa went on. "Your mother was going to bed, and she was leaving you outside to die from the elements. You stood on that porch feeling so helpless and frightened. You did not know what to do. That cold was tearing through your little body."

I put my hands over my eyes and shuddered. I could feel the bitter sting of the cold all over again, sinking into every bone of my unprotected body. Tears began to fall from my eyes as I remembered it. "I collapsed on the porch," I said. "I waited to die."

"God was not going to let you die like that," Little Lisa said. "At that moment, the neighbors arrived home from somewhere. They had been out late that night, and their car pulled into their driveway."

My memory began to fade in and out like a faulty electrical circuit. "I can't see what happened," I said. "I must have gone over to them."

"No," Little Lisa said. "You kept laying in the snow. You wanted to die."

Tears kept falling from my eyes. Only five years old, and I wanted to die. "But I am not dead," I said. "I did not freeze to death there."

"You would have," Little Lisa said. "You did not have any emotional strength within you to alert the neighbors that you were there. I stood up and ran through the snow to them. You could not save yourself, Lisa. You created me to save you."

I gasped at the vision of Little Lisa running through the snow to the neighbor's house. I could see their expression of shock when Little Lisa approached them. The man picked me up and carried me back to my home, where he banged on the door with such force that my mother opened it. She was not going to keep me outside in front of the neighbors. "She must have escaped the house when I wasn't looking," my mother said, without even a hint of guilt in her voice. Once the neighbors were gone, she hit me with her fists and dragged me up the stairs by my hair. She was enraged that I had embarrassed her in front of the neighbors. She threw me onto my bed and then attempted to smother me with my pillow.

"She wanted you dead that night," Little Lisa said.

I saw Little Lisa pick up my leg and kick my mother so hard in the stomach that my mother released the pillow from my face and stumbled away from me. She almost fell, but she caught herself and stood there glaring at me.

Little Lisa glared back at her. They challenged each other with their eyes. A startled look suddenly crossed my mother's face. She may have realized that she had crossed a line that could have left her with a lengthy prison sentence. Abruptly, she turned around and stormed out of my room.

I was not sure what shocked me more—that my mother had tried to destroy me that night, or the fact that Little Lisa had saved my life twice. Even though Little Lisa had saved me, I knew that it was also the moment when I had deemed her the scapegoat for my mother's relentless anger and hatred toward me.

I bent my head between my knees and began to sob. "I am sorry," I told Little Lisa. "I am sorry that I have hated you. I am sorry that I blamed you for the way that my mother treated me. It was easier to blame you than to blame my mother. I was too frightened of my mother to blame her for any of it."

Little Lisa did not respond, but I immediately felt her soften toward me.

"I think that you should talk to your mother about this," Little One said. "It is time for you to confront her about the emotional damage that she has caused you."

"What good would it do now?" I moaned. "It will not change anything that has happened."

"It might help your heart to heal if you let her know how much she has hurt you," Little One said.

I tried to control my sobs as I wiped the tears from my eyes. "She will not care," I said. "She has never cared. She will never change her attitude about me."

"This is not about changing your mother," Little One said. "This is about God helping to change *you.*"

"I am not sure that confronting Lisa's mother would be good for Lisa," Little Lisa said. "It would be one thing if this were the only terrible incident between Lisa and her mother, but there were so many other times. Do you expect Lisa to confront her mother with every memory she will have?"

"Of course not," Little One said. "I think confronting her mother at least once will help start her healing."

"I am not certain Lisa will ever fully heal," Little Lisa said doubtfully.

"The hurt may be raw right now, but wounds always heal," Little One responded.

"Wounds do not always heal," Little Lisa protested. "Some wounds never heal."

"Some people *choose* to keep their wounds open forever," Little One said. "It is a choice that each person must make for themselves."

"I do not think I agree with you," Little Lisa said. "Some wounds never heal, even with the best care."

"Quit with the analogies," I said as I struggled to stop my tears. "I do not want to keep my wounds open for the rest of my life, but these things really hurt. My mother did these things to me. Mothers are supposed to love their children unconditionally."

"It does not always happen that way," Little One said sadly. "You can stay in this place where you are at right now, or you can move forward. That is the choice that you have to make right now."

I wrapped my arms around myself and began to rock back and forth in an unsuccessful attempt to comfort myself. Fresh tears sprang from my eyes as I thought about all of the years that I had tried to please my mother. I would have done anything if it meant she would show me the slightest bit of love. I had worked so hard to be good, to be pleasing to her before the loathing began to creep into my heart. After so many years of trying and failing to please her, I had succumbed to the hatred. It was so much easier to hate than to fail. Now that hate was like a huge lump in my throat that was blocking my ability to breathe. I needed to remove that animosity to restore my breathing before I suffocated to death.

Unable to comfort myself, I felt that hate and rage bubbling to the surface of my heart. Years of trying to be the perfect and responsible child had left me bitter. Also, I was afraid. Even at my age, I still had a deep-rooted fear of my mother and what she might do to me. My fear was like a large tree with rotting roots and a dead trunk. My foundation was unstable, ready to send me to the ground with the slightest gust of wind. I wanted to confront my mother, but I was afraid of the power that I allowed her to have over me.

In my mind's eye, I could see Mouse solemnly looking at me, silently reminding me that God was with me. I wondered how Mouse had developed such a strong faith and trust in God. Whatever faith and trust that Mouse had come directly from me, yet I could not seem to access those strengths that I had given her. I wanted to have the faith and trust in God that she had, but trust was not a safe word for me. Trust was risky. It was safer for me to allow Mouse to do the trusting. I was afraid to trust God. He might hurt me like other people had. He might hurt me like my mother kept hurting me.

Mouse knew my thoughts and fears. She was a part of me, and she knew me almost better than I knew myself. All of my personalities knew certain aspects of me better than I knew them. Mouse wanted to reach out and to take back some of that faith and trust that I had given her, but the fear prevented me from doing so. Did God really love me? Would He love me no matter how worthless I thought I was? If He did love me, could I ever feel safe enough to return His love?

Mouse kept looking at me, trying to will to me the love for God that she felt; that love for God that I had given her but that I could not trust. I stopped crying and began to gulp down the waves of anger rising within my heart. *This is my mother's fault!* I told myself. *She caused me to be this way – she caused me to fear God's love for me!*

I stood up and began to look around the room for my shoes. "All right," I said. "I am going to go talk to her now, before I lose my nerve."

# Nineteen

*Do not hasten in your spirit to be angry, for anger rests in the bosom of fools. (Ecclesiastes 7:9)*

My resolve to confront my mother about her treatment of me strengthened as I made my way to my brother's house. It was a rare occasion that I had ever dared to stand up to her on my own without one of my alters doing it for me. I prayed on the way to Brian's house and asked God to help me keep calm and to guide me as to what to say to her.

When I walked into Brian's house, my prayer to God flew out of the window. My mother was sitting on the couch, drinking beer and watching television. She looked surprised when I stormed into the house unannounced. I ignored how fragile she looked as bitter memories of my childhood spewed like vomit from my brain. So much rage and hurt welled up inside of me that I had a difficult time controlling myself when I looked at her. I envisioned myself wrapping my hands around her throat and squeezing until she took her last breath, and I might have done so if my alters were not struggling to control my body.

From somewhere in my mind I could hear Little One asking God to help me. At that moment, I was as enraged with God as I was with my mother. He had allowed my mother to treat me cruelly for so many years. I was only a child, and God had let my mother do those terrible things to me. He had not stopped her then, so why should He stop me now? I was due my revenge. If God were not going to get vengeance for me, I would do it myself. I could feel my face redden as my blood pressure rose. "Don't you dare ask God to help me!" I screamed at Little One. "He did not help me from being hurt, so He sure does not have to help me now."

A look of confusion crossed my mother's face. She did not know to whom I was talking or why I was yelling. For a moment, I thought I saw fear in her eyes that quickly morphed into annoyance. She was not going to allow herself to show fear. It was an emotion that she would never entertain and especially not over the likes of me. "What are you doing here?" she snapped.

"You tried to kill me when I was five years old!" I shouted. "How many other times did you try to kill me when I was a child?"

"What in the hell are you talking about?" my mother said.

My alters prevented me from moving closer to my mother. I clenched my fists and shook them at her with all of the frustration that I felt. "When I was five years old, you locked me out of the house in the winter with no coat or shoes," I said. "I could have frozen to death, but the neighbors brought me home. After that, you beat me and tried to smother me with a pillow!"

I saw my mother's eyes flicker with an unrecognizable emotion. "I was probably drunk," she said with a casual wave of her hand.

"Does it mean nothing to you?" I shouted.

"Stop yelling and talk to me in a civilized manner," my mother said.

I laughed scornfully. "A civilized manner?" I said. "You never treated me in a civilized manner. You treated me as if I was nothing. You got away with abusing me for years, and now I am crazy because of you. I am here now to exact my revenge on you! You will pay for everything you did to me!"

My mother showed no concern. "What can you do to me now?" she asked calmly.

My mother was right. There wasn't anything that I could do to her that would equal the emotional damage that she had caused me. It would mean nothing to her if I hurt her physically. She had already lost her husband, her son, and her home. As far as she was concerned, her life was already over. Nothing I could do would make her life any worse for her than it was at that moment. Even her health was beginning to fail her. She had nothing left. Slowly, my anger began to cool as I stood there looking at her. Karma—or perhaps God—had already dealt its hand to her. She was miserable. She had always been miserable, but now it could not get any worse for her.

Little One knew what I was thinking. "Vengeance always belongs to God," she said quietly.

I knew that God was not the cause of all of my mother's misery, but it made me feel better to think that He had allowed her to suffer through it all as retribution for me.

My mother sighed and looked away from me. "It is all over now," she said.

I felt my shoulders slump with defeat. "Is that your way of apologizing to me?" I asked.

My mother made no response. She finished her beer and stared at the television with a blank look on her face.

"You have no right to hate me," I said. "You claim that I ruined your life, but you are the one who messed around and got pregnant at sixteen years old. That was not my fault. It is time that you take the blame from me and accept responsibility for your own mistakes."

"I didn't want a child," my mother said.

"I did not ask to be born," I said. "Why didn't you give me up for adoption if you did not want me? I could have lived a better life with parents who wanted me."

"Your Grandparents insisted that I get married and keep you," my mother said. "I tried to lose you. While I was pregnant with you, I wore tight girdles and did what I could to have a miscarriage, but you would not budge."

I closed my eyes and turned my head away from her. Just when I thought she could not possibly hurt me any worse, she always managed to say something even more painful.

"I suppose I can blame your grandparents," my mother said.

I held up my hand. "Stop trying to find somebody to blame," I said. "You are the only one to blame. Even if you did not want me, you had no right to treat me as you did. You took my childhood away from me."

"You took my adult years away from me," my mother retorted.

I was furious with her lack of remorse and her refusal to accept responsibility for her actions. "You ruined me," I accused. "I have mental illness because of you."

"Not only because of me," my mother said. "Your grandfather was the one who sexually abused you."

"You were my mother!" I yelled. "When I told you what he was doing to me, you only blamed me. I was a child who needed protection!"

"So, I will not win the Mother of the Year award," my mother said. "What do you expect me to do about any of it now?"

"An apology would be a good start," I said.

"If I apologized, would it change anything?" my mother asked.

"I know you won't say it," I said. "I have never once heard you apologize to anybody."

My mother and I looked at each other silently for a moment. The hardness had gone out of her eyes and left her looking uncomfortable. I knew that she wanted the conversation to end. There was no sense in keeping it going. Neither of us was going to be a winner. My intense anger toward her had dissipated and had left me feeling tired and defeated. I was proud of myself for having confronted her, but it had not made any difference.

~

Later that night, I poured out the anguish that I was feeling toward God. Since I had not gotten anywhere with my mother, I decided to let Him have my anger for what I had gone through as a child. Why didn't He protect the innocent children in the world? He has the power to do anything He wants to do. Why does He allow some children to suffer such abuse and torment? How could I believe that He loved me when He allowed so much trauma in my life?

"Where were you when I needed you, God?" I railed. "Do you expect me to forgive my mother when she won't even so much as apologize to me? That is not fair. I am not the one who did wrong in this situation!"

It was not God who answered my cry; it was Little One. "I do not think any human can ever understand why God allows the suffering that He allows," she said. "But what we do know is that God will work everything out for good to those who trust Him."

"Really?" I raged at her. "What good has come out of all of the suffering that I did as a child? Is it good that I now have so much emotional damage and emotional issues?"

"Perhaps one day God will use your suffering to draw other people to Him," Little One mused.

"Do not hand me that line," I said. "I did not ask for God to use me. I would rather have had a happy childhood with parents who loved me."

"Evil and sin have infected the world because God lovingly allows people free will," Little One said. "Do not blame God for what people do. Do not stay focused on this earthly life, Lisa. In the Bible, Paul states that the sufferings of this life are nothing compared to the glory that you will one day receive in eternal life."

"Tell that to all of the abused and dying children in this world," I said bitterly.

"I do not have all of the answers," Little One sighed. "I only know that God is good, and He can make sense of your life if you look to Him. You are not the only one that has suffered. Think of how much Jesus suffered for you. God also allowed Jesus to suffer, and Jesus accepted His suffering willingly and out of love. At the end of His great suffering, God restored Him to full glory. But even Jesus had to suffer first and then wait for His restoration." She paused and then added, "Don't forget the story of Job. Nothing can compare to the suffering that Job did in this life, but God restored Him in the end as well. God will eventually restore every one of His people who suffer in this life. You need to keep the faith that in the end, God will make every wrong in this world right. That is why He left His people the promises in Revelation 21. There will come a time when you will not even remember any of your earthly sufferings. Those who endure this life will be richly rewarding by our loving God. That is what faith and trust in Him are all about. So, don't blame Him for the terrible things that your family has done to you."

"I do not blame Him for what they did, I blame Him for not stopping it," I said. "I know that He gave people free will because He does not want people to be forced to love Him or forced to be His robots. However, right now I still feel angry with Him. Whether it is wrong or right, please do not invalidate my anger."

"I am sure that God understands that you feel angry with Him," Little One said. "I know that God hurt as much or even more than you did about the things that happened to you. Just trust that He will one day make everything right for you."

"I thought life would get easier if I had God on my side," I said. "I thought that He would fix everything for me. I did not think I would have to continue to struggle. I thought He would heal my emotional issues and that I would finally have a happy life. I feel like God is letting me down." I was ready to throw in the towel and collapse on my knees before God.

"Lisa, nowhere in the Bible does God promise us an easy life on this side of heaven," Little One said. "Jesus warns us that there will be hardship and much trouble in this life. What He does promise is to always be with us and to help us through those difficult times."

I covered my face with my hands. "I am not certain that is enough for me," I wailed. "I want more from God than just helping me through difficult times. I do not want there to be any more times that are difficult. I have already had my share of them." I uncovered my face and sighed. "I know that God has promised me eternal life and a new earth to live on," I said. "I try to hang onto those future promises, but isn't there something good that He can give me *now?*"

"He has already given you His beloved Son," Little One said. "How can you ask for anything more than that? He has given you salvation and forgiveness."

"I am not asking for material wealth," I said hastily. "I do not mean to tell God that giving me His Son is not enough for me." My face turned scarlet as I struggled to find the correct words.

"I know what you want from God," Mouse spoke up. "What you are seeking is peace and joy in your mind and heart."

"That is right!" I exclaimed. "I would like to have peace and joy no matter what difficult times I may be facing."

"God would be happy to give you peace and joy," Mouse assured me.

"Well, I have been waiting," I said. "Where are they? When is God going to give them to me?"

"Peace and joy come with faith and trust," Mouse said. "They go hand in hand. The more faith and trust you develop, the more peace and joy you will have."

"Why does God have to make some things so difficult?" I moaned.

"God does not make things difficult. People do," Mouse corrected. "The gospel message is simple."

"Faith and trust are not simple," I said.

"For me, they are," Mouse said.

"I gave you that faith and trust you have," I reminded her.

"That is right," Mouse agreed. "So, take some of it back from me now and see how good it can be."

"Mouse, do you remember that Scripture you once read to me about how if you cannot love your brother whom you can see, how can you love God whom you cannot see?" I asked.

"Sure," Mouse said.

"By the same token, if I cannot trust people that I can see, then how can I trust in a God that I cannot see? So many people have broken their promises to me."

"God is not just another person," Mouse replied. "Tell me what promise He has made in His word that He has broken."

I rubbed my head as I thought about it. "I cannot think of anything off the top of my head," I admitted.

"That is because there isn't any," Mouse said. "I defy you to find one promise from the Bible that He has failed. Some of His promises have not been delivered yet, but you can be assured that they will be fulfilled. His track record has been perfect thus far."

I sat back and thought about that. Mouse had made a great point.

"God may not have stopped what happened to you as a child," Mouse said quietly, "but God can use anything for good if we ask Him to. He can use any circumstance for His glory. All you have to do is believe that He loves you and trust Him."

"For people like me that is easier said than done," I sighed, but I was trying to find my way.

# Twenty

*I would have lost heart, unless I had believed that I would see the goodness of the Lord in the land of the living. (Psalm 27:13)*

My mother had been living with my brother for three years when she started expressing the desire to have her own apartment. Brian was going to get married, and she felt that she would be intruding on his growing family. Neither Brian nor I thought that she would do well on her own and we spent ample time trying to talk her out of it. Our pleading did not dissuade her. She had never lived on her own, and she insisted she wanted to try it.

With much reluctance, Brian helped her move into a small apartment about ten minutes away from his home. He and I set her up with the furnishings that she needed, and I went grocery shopping for her. My relationship with her was still tense, but I did all that I could to get her set up and comfortable in her new place.

For the first two weeks that my mother lived alone, she seemed to do okay. I went to her apartment for a couple of hours every day to make sure that she was taking care of herself and to clean and do errands for her. The emotional tension between us began to ease a little bit with each day that I went there. She started to share stories with me about my family and her childhood. Soon I realized that I was staying with her longer than necessary because I enjoyed listening to her relate tales about my ancestors that I would never have heard otherwise. I began to hang out with her to watch television and cook meals for her. Although my mother was not good about expressing her gratitude, I had a sense that she appreciated me being there.

Whenever an opportunity would lend itself, I talked to my mother about God and salvation. She was not always willing to listen, but sometimes she was, and I made the most of those times. I still had regrets about having not made sure that my father and my brother had known enough about salvation before they passed away, and I did not want to be left with the additional burden of not having shared it with my mother. Even though she did not always seem interested, I prayed that God would open her heart and would help her to understand His mercy. I often felt inadequate whenever I talked to her about God, because I was still struggling to understand my place with Him, but I witnessed to her in the best ways that I could, and I hoped that God would be pleased with my effort. My heart was still somewhat hard and unforgiving toward my mother, but I did not want her to miss spending eternity with God, even if it meant I would also be spending eternity with her.

Two weeks after my mother moved into her apartment, my mother asked me if I would be going to church service that weekend. "Yes, I am going," I replied. "Why do you ask?"

My mother hesitated and looked uncomfortable. "I thought I might go with you this weekend," she said before hastily adding, "if I wake up in time."

I was so stunned that for a moment I could not speak. I knew that if I made a big deal out of itshe would change her mind, so I tried to temper the excitement that I was feeling. "Sure," I said. "I will stop by here in the morning on my way there."

"I am not getting dressed up, and I am not giving them any money," my mother said.

"You do not have to," I assured her.

"I am only going to get out of this apartment for a while," my mother said. "I have not been to a church service since I was a child, and even then, I only went once or twice."

"The church that I go to is not like a Catholic church," I warned her. "My church is a more modern church. People at my church wear jeans and T-shirts, and the music is loud." I picked up a sponge and began to wipe the stove. I was still trying to act casually about her going, but I felt anxious because I wanted to make it a good experience for her. "Would you rather I take you to a Catholic church?" I asked.

My mother shook her head. "Wherever you go will be fine," she said.

~

When Sunday morning came, I was certain that my mother would have changed her mind about going to church. When I arrived at her apartment, I found her sitting at her kitchen table, dressed in black jeans and a flowered shirt, drinking coffee and smoking a cigarette. I was relieved that she was not drinking alcohol as she usually did in the morning.

For the first time in my life, I was impressed with my mother that morning. She walked into church confidently and greeted the people with a smile and a handshake. She listened to the pastor's sermon with rapt attention. I could hardly believe that it was the same woman who had abused and embarrassed me for most of my life. She conducted herself so well that I was almost proud of her.

"What did you think of the service?" I asked her after it was over, and we were headed home.

"I think I went deaf from the music," my mother replied. "But I liked the sermon, and the people seemed nice."

"Would you be willing to go again?" I asked eagerly.

"Do not get your hopes up," my mother said. "I am not going to turn into a religious person. I just wanted to see what it was about." She paused and then added, "I might go back for Christmas or Easter service."

That was good enough for me. I would take anything from her at that point, no matter how small of a nugget it was.

As I pulled into the parking lot at her apartment building and shut off the car, I could hear a faint rattling sound coming from my mother's chest. I noticed she was having some trouble catching her breath. I reached out to her and asked, "What is wrong?"

My mother pushed my hand away. "I am fine," she said, but it seemed difficult for her to speak.

"You don't sound fine," I frowned. I knew that my mother had been diagnosed with a lung disease called COPD many years before, but she refused to stop her heavy smoking. Her doctor had wanted her to start using oxygen the year before, but she had refused that as well. "It looks as if you need to take your doctor's advice and start using oxygen," I told her.

"That is a pain in the rear," my mother said.

"But you are having trouble breathing," I said. "Do you want me to take you to the hospital?"

"I said I am fine," my mother snapped, and I could hear the annoyance in her voice. "Just help me inside. After I get some rest, I will be okay."

I grasped my mother's arm as she walked slowly into her apartment. She gasped for breath the entire time. Once inside, she fell into a chair and lowered her head between her knees. After a few minutes, she managed to take a deep breath. She lifted her head and looked at me. "I am okay now," she said.

She was breathing better, but I was still concerned. "You need to start using oxygen," I said.

My mother gave me a warning look. "Leave me alone about it," she said. "Don't ruin an otherwise good morning."

"I am concerned about you," I said, and I was surprised to find that my concern for her was genuine.

My mother looked down at her hands. "Why should you be concerned about me?" she asked.

"I just am," I replied.

"I don't deserve for you to be concerned about me," my mother said.

For a few minutes after my mother said that, she and I were rooted silently in our places, me watching her look at her hands. A moment was passing between us. I knew that she was trying to acknowledge the emotional damage that she had caused me over so many years.

I held back my tears as I swallowed a lump of sadness thick in my throat. I wanted to tell her that everything was okay between us, but I could not do it. At that point, it would not have been true for me. I realized then that my hatred toward my mother had softened, but now she felt like a stranger to me. Without the hate, I did not know what to feel for her.

I finally found my voice. "If you are okay now, I am going to go home," I said.

"I have an appointment with the foot doctor at noon tomorrow," my mother said.

"I will be here tomorrow to take you," I said.

As I started for the door, my mother called my name. I stopped, but I kept my back to her, and I waited.

"I am sorry, Lisa," my mother said quietly. "I am sorry for what I have done to you."

I heard my heart beating rapidly in my ears. It was the vindication that I had waited for my entire life. It had finally happened. My mother had apologized for hurting me and for hating me. She was taking responsibility for her actions. God was presenting me with the start of my healing.

I did not turn around to face my mother. I kept my back to her, but I am sure that she could see my shoulders shaking. "I forgive you," I said.

The next day when I returned to her apartment, I found my mother floor in full cardiac arrest.

I found my mother on her living room floor with her upper back against her recliner and her head slumped to her chest. I called out to her, but she did not respond. With my heart racing, I reached out and felt her face and her arms. Her skin was warm, but I could see that she was not breathing. I felt her wrist for a pulse, but my hands were shaking so badly that I was not able to tell if I could feel her heart beating. I felt her neck and was crushed when I realized that both her heart and her breathing had ceased.

"Mom!" I screamed. I grabbed her by her frail shoulders and laid her flat on the floor. I had no idea how long she had been in cardiac arrest, but I thought since her body was still warm, there might be a chance that I could save her. I had taken a CPR course many years before when I had worked at the nursing home, so I knew what to do. I tilted her head back, pinched her nose, grasped her chin, and blew twice into her mouth. I was vaguely aware of the taste of stale cigarettes and alcohol on her mouth. I ignored the unpleasant taste and kept going. I pumped her chest thirty times before blowing into her mouth two more times. Her chest rose slightly, and I wondered if she was able to get any oxygen into her damaged lungs.

"Come on mom…come on!" I cried out as I continued to blow into her mouth and pump her chest. After I had done it for several cycles, I pulled my cell phone from my pocket and dialed 911 for rescue. I continued doing CPR on my mother while I waited for the paramedics. It was hard work. After a few minutes, my arms were sore, and beads of sweat formed on my forehead. Adrenaline and determination kept me going.

I begged God not to let her die, not when forgiveness was just beginning to penetrate my heart, not when I was ready to make some good memories with her to combat all the bad ones. For most of my life, I had wished my mother dead, but now I was on my knees, desperately trying to keep her alive. I was the one she had tortured and traumatized, and now I was the one blowing life-giving oxygen into her failing lungs.

"Please give me the strength to keep going, God!" I pleaded, and He did give me the strength. I kept going, pumping her chest, breathing into her mouth, pleading for her life.

Suddenly I heard a gasp from my mother. It sounded like a snort, and it frightened me. She was not breathing correctly; she was just snorting every few seconds. She was still unresponsive, but when I felt her neck again, I thought I felt a few faltering beats of her heart.

"I am sorry I wished you were dead," I sobbed as I continued to press her chest. "You are the only mother I will ever have. I only wanted you to love me."

By the time the paramedics arrived and took over, I was exhausted, both mentally and physically. I was unable to tell the paramedics what had happened to my mother, but I did share her medical conditions with them.

One of the paramedics noticed an empty prescription bottle laying on the floor next to my mother. He picked it up and glanced at the label. "Pain medication," he said. "It was filled four days ago, but it is empty now."

"She does abuse her prescription medications," I said. "She is addicted to both pain and anxiety medications."

"This looks like a drug overdose," the paramedic said.

As the paramedics whisked my mother to the hospital, I called Brian to let him know what had happened. Together we rode to the hospital. Shortly after we arrived there, a doctor told us that my mother was going to be put into the Intensive Care Unit on life support. She had over dosed on her prescription medication and was in a coma. He also told us that she had likely suffered brain damage and that her odds for survival were very slim.

When I finally went in to see my mother, I nearly collapsed from overwhelming sadness. She had a thick breathing tube in her throat, and she was hooked up to several different machines. Her face and hands were grotesquely swollen. I pulled up a chair and sat next to her bed. I could not stop staring at her. I could not believe that God was going to let her die without allowing me to have one final conversation with her. Forgiveness had started for me, but there were still many unspoken words between us.

For six days, my mother lingered in a coma while her condition only continued to worsen. Her body temperature spiked all the way up to 108 degrees, and the doctor said it would leave her brain damaged if it wasn't damaged already. I kept vigil next to her bed and prayed that God would allow me to talk to her one more time.

After six days, the doctor deemed my mother hopeless, and he began to talk to Brian and me about removing her breathing tube and allowing her to pass away peacefully. There was nothing more they could do for her.

We were told that if she ever awoke from her coma, she would be in a vegetative state.

Removing my mother from life support was one of the most difficult decisions I have ever had to make in my life. Finally, Brian and I decided that the most merciful thing to do for her would be to allow her to pass away. There were too many factors working against her survival. The doctor removed her breathing tube and informed us that she would not survive the night. I sat next to her bed, and with a heavy heart, I waited for the saga between my mother and me to finally end.

The next morning, I was still waiting for my mother to pass away.

When the doctor arrived that morning, he was stunned that not only had my mother survived the night, she was also breathing normally on her own. "Her vital signs are better this morning," he said. "Her fever is going down. I do not know what this means for her."

I looked at my mother. Her eyes were darting back and forth behind her eyelids. Suddenly her eyes briefly fluttered open and then closed again.

The doctor looked astonished. He clutched my mother's chart against his chest and asked me, "Do you believe in God?"

"Yes sir, I do," I said.

"The only explanation that I have for your mother's current condition is that it is a miracle," the doctor said. "Your mother may regain consciousness. However, I still do not know the extent of the damage to her brain. She may not be able to speak. She may not recognize you."

I nodded and bent over my mother so that I was close to her face. "Can you hear me, mom?" I said. "It's Lisa. I am here with you."

"Do not expect much from her," the doctor said. "Please alert the nurse right away if there is any further change in her condition."

I nodded again. Once the doctor had left the room, I sat next to my mother and began to talk to her. I rambled on about unimportant topics, such as the weather and how well I thought the hospital staff was doing with her care. Every so often, her eyes would open and close. I became encouraged when I saw her hand move slightly. I did not know if she could understand what I was saying to her, but I thought it was important that she know I was there.

Two hours after my mother first opened her eyes, she opened them and kept them open. She struggled to focus on me. Her mouth began to move, and she tried to speak to me.

"Take it easy," I said to her as I pulled the cord to call the nurse.

My mother lifted her hand and weakly gestured me to move closer to her. I turned my ear towards her mouth. "Do you know who I am?" I asked hopefully.

My mother's voice was weak and faltering, but I could understand her words. "Lisa," she said, "for God's sake, shut your mouth for a while. You are giving me a headache."

I rested my head on the bed rail and began to sob great waves of relief. God had answered my prayers and had graciously allowed me another chance to connect with my mother. I was going to make certain that I did not waste that chance.

# Twenty-one

*O wretched man that I am! Who will deliver me*
*from this body of death? I thank God – through*
*Jesus Christ our Lord! So then, with the mind I*
*myself serve the law of God, but with the flesh the*
*law of sin. (Romans 7:24-25)*

My mother suffered no brain damage from her overdose, but it took a great toll on her already weakened physical condition. She lost what little muscle strength she had in her legs and was confined to a wheelchair. Her lungs were further damaged by the incident, and she was tethered to an oxygen tank around the clock. She was moved from the hospital to a nursing home under the guise of receiving physical therapy, but I was certain that her health would not improve. I was relieved when she went into the nursing home because I knew that her propensity to abuse her prescription medications would be controlled.

I had a strong sense that my time with my mother was limited. I went to the nursing home nearly every day and made sure that she was receiving good care, and that she had everything that she wanted or needed. My mother and I spent those hours talking and getting to know each other in ways that we never had before. It was the first time I had ever spent time with her without the effects of alcohol or pill abuse dictating our time together. I was amazed to find that my mother was not the monster that I thought she was. Underneath the layers of substance abuse and hostility, my mother had some decent qualities. I was grateful to God that He had given me the chance to find those qualities.

My mother and I both knew that she was soon going to die. Her health continued to decline, and eventually, she began to bleed from her mouth with what turned out to be oral cancer. In a short matter of time, the cancer spread to her salivary glands. Her doctor determined that her body was not strong enough to withstand any cancer treatment and the only thing to do was let the disease run its course. She had a couple of months left to live at best. I knew that there would be no more chances for my mother and I. God was going to take her this time. Whatever we said to each other during those final weeks was what I was going to have to remember her.

"I am sorry that I ruined your life," I told her one day while I was visiting her. "I am sorry that I was born." It seemed like neither of us could stop apologizing once we had started.

My mother was holding a Kleenex against her mouth to try to stop the tumor inside of it from bleeding. It was difficult for her to speak, but she was determined to do so. She said something then that I thought I would never hear. She threw her Kleenex into the trash can and said, "Lisa, my miserable life was not your fault. I used you as a scapegoat."

"You hated me," I said.

My mother shook her head and reached for another Kleenex. "The truth is that I was jealous of you," she said.

I pushed the Kleenex box closer to her. "Jealous?" I said with surprise. "Why would you be jealous of me?"

"I was sixteen years old when I became pregnant with you," my mother explained. "I was very immature. When you were born, my parents fell in love with you immediately. You were the apple of their eye. They lavished you with the love and affection that they had never given me. I was jealous of you."

My mother's revelation stunned me, and I did not know how to respond. I waited for her to continue.

"I also resented that my parents insisted I quit school and marry your father," my mother went on. "It was not what I wanted for my life. It was easier for me to take out my resentment on you rather than to admit my mistakes or show anger toward my parents. I never really hated you. I hated myself. My anger toward you was misplaced. I am sorry, but I cannot take back any of the cruel things that I said or did to you. The only thing that you can do is to try to move past it."

At that moment, I felt liberated. A heavy burden was lifted from my soul. Her words did not eradicate the memories of all that she had done to me, but it lifted most of the pain that went along with those memories. I knew that it might take a long time for me to recover from the emotional damage that she had caused me. "What about all of those times when you called me worthless and ugly?" I asked.

"That is how I felt about myself," my mother admitted. "I was looking into a mirror every time that I looked at you."

"I am grateful that you told me this," I said. "I have so much healing to do, but this is a start. You have put a Band-Aid over a gaping wound in my heart."

My mother put her head on her pillow and closed her eyes. "I don't want to die," she murmured.

"Are you afraid?" I asked.

"I am afraid of facing the things that I have done in my life," my mother responded quietly.

"You do not have to fear it if you get right with God," I said.

My mother opened her eyes and looked at me but said nothing.

"I have told you how to get right with God," I reminded her. "You have to accept Jesus as your Savior."

"I know that," my mother said.

I leaned over and grasped my mother's hand. "Please get right with God," I said. "I want to be certain that you and I will spend eternity together."

My mother glanced at my hand clasped with hers. "Do not worry about where I stand with God," she said. "Worry about where you stand with Him."

"But how will I know where you went after you die?" I asked. "I do not want to spend the rest of my life wondering where you are like I do with Dad and Donnie. I feel so much guilt about them. I think that I did not witness well enough to them. I did not say enough about God to them."

"Listen to me, Lisa." My mother's voice was firm. "You have spent your entire life thinking that my life was your responsibility. Do not spend the rest of your life thinking that my relationship with God—or anybody else's relationship with Him—is also your responsibility. Once you tell a person about God and salvation, it is between that person and God. Whatever your father and brother chose to do about their relationship with God was their decision, not yours. Whatever I choose to do is not your responsibility. I am an adult, and it is my choice." She closed her eyes again. "I can at least leave you with that much," she said.

My mother passed away a few weeks after that conversation. I did not know how to feel after she died. I felt void of emotion as I got into my car and took a long drive to clear my head. For most of my life, I had wanted my mother gone. Now she was gone, and I did not know whether to feel relieved or sad.

After driving for an hour, I pulled into a rest stop and turned off my car. I realized that I was void of emotion because I was in shock that she was gone. As I sat there trying to process her death, my shock gave way to grief, and I dissolved into hysterical tears. My mother had died. She was gone from this earth. The abuse and trauma were officially over, but so was the truce that we had formed with one another. I did not know if I would ever be with her again. For the first time, I wanted my mother. A raw and unprotected need for love and comfort from my mother flowed from the depths of my heart. The fear of never being with my mother again caused me so much agony that I began to cry out to God for peace and relief.

Through my tears, a vision of light flickered beside me. I turned my head and was thunderstruck by what I saw there. Hovering over the empty passenger seat was a bright yellow ball of light about the size of a tennis ball. Radiating from the shimmering light was the greatest sense of peace and love that I had ever felt. Comfort and love surrounded me like a warm blanket on a cold night. My grief disappeared and was replaced with awe as I gazed at that ball of beautiful warm light. I could feel my mother's presence. I had the sense that she was telling me everything was going to be all right. She was with God, and she was happy. She was not sick anymore, and she was full of love and peace. I knew that I would see her again, and relief washed over me in waves.

That shimmering ball of light only lasted for a few seconds and then disappeared, but the strong feelings of love and comfort remained draped over me. My life long weary soul felt refreshed and alive. My mother's presence was gone, but it was replaced by the presence of God's Holy Spirit. The tension in my body dribbled away as a thought formed in my mind: *I am valuable to God, and He loves me.*

*God loves me!*

In my mind, I could see Jesus, bloody and battered, carrying a heavy wooden cross on his back. He was willingly enduring a brutal and painful death so that I could be reconciled with His Holy Father. He had endured crucifixion so that God could look past my sins and see me with love, mercy, and forgiveness.

Jesus died for me! God let His precious Son die because of His great love for me!

"My Lord and My God," I cried out as I wrapped my arms around myself and cried tears that were soaked with gratitude toward God. "Thank you for forgiving me. Thank you for sending your Son to save me. Thank you for loving me enough to do that for me."

At that moment, I finally understood how God saw me. I was not worthless to Him. He did not see me in the negative way that I was made to feel about myself for so many years. I was more valuable to Him than silver and gold, but I was a sinner. He is so Holy that all sin, no matter how small it may be, deeply offends Him. I had thought in ways and behaved in ways that offended such a Holy God, and I needed His forgiveness. Not only did I need His forgiveness, but I also desired that forgiveness more than anything else. I wanted to be right with God. I wanted my name to be written in His Book of Life so that I would not miss any of the future promises that He made for those who love Him. He had made a way for me and for everybody else who desired to be right with Him to be forgiven. He had made that one perfect blood sacrifice that would be enough to abolish sin forever. He had allowed His son to die in my place. Jesus had taken the punishment that I so deserved. He had taken my punishment to give me eternal life with God.

"Jesus, thank you for sacrificing yourself for me," I sobbed. "Thank you for showing me what forgiveness truly is by leading me to forgive my mother. I have forgiven my mother just as God the Father has forgiven me. I accept your death as the perfect sacrifice for my sins. I know that I will not be perfect. Please send the Holy Spirit to fill my heart and to help me to know when I sin and to help me have a clean heart."

I lifted my eyes and looked around me. The colors of the world seemed exceptionally bright, and my heart felt light. My life had been difficult up until that point, and I knew that I would continue to face hard times. God never promised that His people would have an easy life on this earth. What He does promise is to always be with us, and to help us through the difficult times. I might never understand why God allowed me to endure so much abuse and trauma as a child, or why I would have to struggle with so many emotional and mental issues as an adult. The reasons why no longer mattered to me. What did matter was that in the end, God has a glorious future in store for those who have endured the difficulties of this earthly life. There will come a day when He will make all of the wrong things right.

My alters were silent while my new awareness of God's love and grace was happening to me, but they were all feeling the same joy that I was. "Congratulations, Lisa," Mouse said. "God's salvation has finally moved from your head to your heart."

# Twenty-two

*That if you confess with your mouth the Lord Jesus*
*and believe in your heart that God has raised Him*
*from the dead, you will be saved. (Romans 10:9)*

Carrying a bouquet of brightly colored flowers for my mother, I made my way to the cemetery where my family members were interred. Gently I laid the flowers on the ground, then I stepped back to look at their niches. First my mother, followed by my father, and then Donnie at the end of the row. They were gone from this earth, but I knew that they still existed somewhere. "May God have mercy on you all," I said quietly.

At that moment, a cardinal came along and perched on the top of my mother's niche. It looked at me for a moment and then flew away, a beautiful drop of red against a cloudless blue sky.

I wiped a tear from my cheek as I gazed at my mother's niche. Her name, along with her birth and death dates, glittered on the marbled granite door. I had forgiven my mother, and in turn, I had found God's forgiveness for myself.

"I love you," I whispered, and then with Little One, Little Lisa, Mouse and Bug solidly beside me, strengthening me, I headed home.

~

"Wake up everybody!" Mouse yelled excitedly the next morning. "He is risen!"

Easter morning dawned early on a beautiful spring day the year after my mother passed away. I woke up feeling joy at being able to celebrate the resurrection of Jesus.

"I will make us a grand holiday breakfast before we go to church," Little Lisa said cheerfully as we climbed out of bed to start our day.

"This is the most important day of the year for me," I said as we sat down to a feast of pancakes, scrambled eggs, and sausage.

Bug reached across the table for sausage and dragged her bare arm across of plate of syrup in the process. She attempted to wipe the sticky syrup from her arm with a paper towel. "Why?" she asked, as she shoved a sausage link into her eager mouth.

"Today is the day that we celebrate the resurrection of Jesus," I explained. "Today we commemorate Him rising from the dead."

"Is His rising from the dead more important than His birth?" Bug asked.

I pondered over Bug's question for a moment. "They were both very important events," I said. "But Jesus rising from the dead is what gives us the hope and promise of eternal life after we die."

"For those who believe in Him and accept Him as their Savior," Mouse added.

"Right," I agreed.

Bug was not finished with her questions. "Did Jesus go to hell while He was dead for three days?" she asked.

"There are differences of opinion about that," I said. "Some think that Jesus' death itself was sufficient as a sacrifice for our sins and that He went right to paradise when He died. Others think that because He was taking the punishment for our sins, He went to hell for those three days because that is where we as sinners deserve to go."

"What do you think happened to Jesus after He died?" Bug asked.

"I think that Jesus took our entire punishment for sin, and that included being separated from God for a time and going to hell," I replied.

Bug nodded and shoved another sausage link into her mouth.

We rushed through breakfast because I wanted to go to the earliest church service. My church was no longer meeting in the gymnasium of the high school as a large building had been completed the year before. As I walked into the church that morning, the building was filled with the sound of beautiful upbeat music, and the smell of fragrant lilies filled the air.

I made my way to the sanctuary and sat in one of the pews. The church was crowded with people, but my eyes were drawn to the huge wooden cross standing at the front of the sanctuary. A light white cloth was draped over the cross, and a small spotlight from the ceiling shone down on it. Tears sprang to my eyes as I gazed at it. *For the wages of sin is death, but the gift of God is eternal life in Christ Jesus our Lord.* Romans 6:23.

As I waited for the service to begin, I thought about all that had happened to me over the years and how my life had changed since my mother's death. My circumstances were still the same. I still had emotional difficulties to work through, and I still needed medication and therapy for my mental illnesses. I also still had financial issues to struggle with. The difference was that I now faced those difficulties with strength and hope that I never had before. Those difficulties paled in comparison to the glorious future that I now know God has in store for me, starting with His most precious gift of salvation. *For by grace you have been saved through faith, and that not of yourselves; it is the gift of God.* Ephesians 2:8.

*Praise the Lord! Oh, give thanks to the Lord, for He is good! For His mercy endures forever.* Psalm 106:1.

Made in the USA
Monee, IL
28 December 2019